THE
LOW FAT
COOKBOOK

THE
LOW FAT
COOKBOOK

SUE KREITZMAN

Photography by Ian O'Leary

Food styling by Janice Murfitt

COVENT
GARDEN
BOOKS

A DORLING KINDERSLEY BOOK

Art Editor
Sue Storey

Editor
Janice Anderson

Assistant Editor
Lorraine Turner

DTP Designer
Bridget Roseberry

Managing Editor
Mary Ling

Deputy Art Director
Carole Ash

Production Manager
Maryann Rogers

Production Controller
Manjit Sihra

For Freda

First published in Great Britain in 1998
by Dorling Kindersley Limited,
9 Henrietta Street, London WC2E 8PS
This edition published in 1999 for Covent Garden Books
Visit us on the World Wide Web
at http://www.dk.com

A CIP catalogue for this book is available from the British Library

ISBN 187185 431 8

Reproduced in Singapore by Colourscan
Printed and bound in China

CONTENTS

INTRODUCTION 6

GALLERY
OF LOW FAT DISHES 10

*A mouthwatering array of dishes for all
kinds of meal, rich in colour, bursting with
flavour and amazingly low in fat*

LOW FAT ESSENTIALS 26

How to take the fat out of cooking, with step-by-step photographs of the key techniques

RECIPES 44

A spectacular collection of more than 150 inspiring easy-to-make low-fat recipes, each with a nutritional analysis detailing fat and cholesterol content

INTRODUCTION

HOW I LOVE FOOD! Vivid colour, interesting texture, bombastic flavour and lots of pizzazz – I want it all. My expertise centres on low-fat cooking, the result of an almost lifetime battle with obesity coupled with my enduring passion for food in all its glorious and fascinating aspects. My philosophy is no added fat – I don't believe in substituting one high-fat regime for another – and my aim is to help you achieve a total low-fat, high nutrition gastronomic lifestyle.

I'm not the food police, however; you must come to a health-giving low-fat way-of-life of your own volition. An enforced, unimaginative spell of low-fat eating against one's will means cottage cheese, naked slabs of steamed fish and grilled chicken breasts, piles of raw vegetables and undressed salads, and no puddings at all. The result? Dreadful boredom followed, often, by a desperate urge to binge.

MAKING A LOW-FAT LIFESTYLE ENJOYABLE

Nutrition without sensual enjoyment is grim indeed; healthy eating must be a celebration, not a punishment. You will not find a lengthy, scientifically based explanation of fats here: all you need to know about fats and the place of cholesterol in the diet is in Fat Facts (see pages 162–3).

Successful low-fat cooking depends on technique. That is why this book emphasizes technique above all, not just in the Techniques sections (see pages 28–37), but throughout the recipe sections. I want you to be able to apply these techniques generally to all your cooking, not just to the specific recipes I have chosen for this book.

If you take on board the oil-water spray, the stock sauté, the flavour infusions, the sauces from vegetable purées and so on, a low-fat kitchen lifestyle becomes easy and natural. Above all, your meals will be a pleasurable, well-rounded fiesta of vegetables, fruits, grains, fish, lean meat and poultry, with the emphasis on the vegetables, fruit and grains. You will find lots of sauces, salsas, garnishes and embellishments made from vegetables and fruit. They add colour, excitement and plenty of wonderful nutrition. I always want my recipes to resonate with big, round, intense flavours and fragrances. The lack of added fat means that the cloying, blunting quality of those fats (and oils) is gone.

THE INTELLIGENT OPTION?

There are many reasons for embracing a low-fat way of life. It is an intelligent, healthy and fulfilling method of weight control and weight maintenance, of course, but it goes far beyond that. Low dietary fat levels are a necessity for those who suffer from assorted medical problems, heart and artery disease, high blood cholesterol levels, diabetes and gall bladder problems among them, but they have also become a lifetime food regime of choice for those enlightened people who want a healthier, thoroughly modern, lighter way of eating.

Now that we are nearly at the end of the twentieth century, heavy, fat-based, greasy and cloying food seems hopelessly outdated. Those who want a fresh vibrancy to their meals, who want to dine well yet not end a meal feeling bilious, bloated and weighed down, and who want to prevent later problems with obesity and fat-related diseases, turn to lowered fat levels with

great relief and enthusiasm. Suddenly, those reactionary chefs and foodies who continue to cling tenaciously to their old, fat-based techniques seem sadly obsolete and misguided. So enjoy the present, and look forward to a healthy and gastronomically rewarding future. Revel in the goodness of a low-fat, full-flavour lifestyle, easily achieved when you follow my basic cooking techniques and use (and adapt to your own tastes) the recipes here.

NUTRITIONAL ANALYSIS

Some recipes in this book are extremely low in fat, some are reduced fat. A sensible low-fat diet will derive approximately 20–25 per cent of total calories from fat. That works out to about 50 grams of fat per day. All recipes have a nutritional analysis giving an idea of what the fat levels actually are, but remember:

The analyses accompanying the recipes are only approximate: nutrient levels in food can vary from time to time and from place to place, and are not standard.

Sometimes, the figures for saturated and unsaturated fats do not equal the total fat figure. This is because the fat total includes, as well as fatty acids, other non-fatty acid materials.

The symbol "<1g" in the analyses means the recipe quantity analyzed contains less than 1 gram of the fat named. "Neg" ("negligible") means 0.1g or 0.2g of fat.

There is no need to turn mealtimes into grim accounting sessions. Use my techniques wherever possible, cut out high-fat foods and added fats from your meals, and your fat levels will fall very neatly into place.

COOKERY NOTES

1 All recipes are written in imperial and metric measurements. Use one or the other, but do not mix measurements.

2 Teaspoons and tablespoons are level: 1tsp = 5ml, 1tbsp = 15ml. Eggs, when used (which is not often) are large.

3 Appetites and meal "shapes" vary, so take the portion sizes as a general suggestion and adjust to your needs.

4 Because ovens vary greatly, oven timings given in recipes can only be approximate. Always preheat the oven. For fan-assisted ovens, reduce the oven temperature by about 20°F (see the manufacturer's instructions for your oven).

GALLERY
of
LOW FAT
DISHES

THE RICHLY COLOURFUL PHOTOGRAPHS ON THESE

PAGES SHOW HOW GORGEOUS LOW-FAT FOOD CAN LOOK.

OF COURSE, TO FIND OUT JUST HOW GREAT IT

CAN TASTE, YOU MUST MAKE THE RECIPES FOR YOURSELF.

THERE IS PLENTY OF CHOICE: PAGES OF POULTRY

AND FISH DISHES, TORTILLA FILLINGS, PIZZAS AND PASTA

DISHES, OFFERING ALL THE AUTHENTIC FLAVOURS OF

TRADITIONAL VERSIONS, PLUS MANY EXCITING NEW IDEAS

FOR TOPPINGS AND SAUCES. AND THERE ARE DREAMY

DESSERTS, WHERE LAYERS OF FRUITS MINGLE ENTICINGLY

WITH DELICATELY FLAVOURED CREAM TOPPINGS.

PIZZAS

Opposite:
TOMATO &
MOZZARELLA
(See page 145)

Per serving	Low fat	Full fat
Total fat (g)	10	60
Calories	700	1182

GOOEY MELTED CHEESE, tender cloves of pan-braised garlic, garden-fresh herbs, earthy wild mushrooms, silky sautéed peppers, olive- and chilli-flecked tomato sauce, juicy tomatoes bursting with flavour, all piled on to a crisp, freshly baked yeast dough, make irresistible party fare for family and friends.

"Food ... lovingly prepared, and eaten in good company, warms the being with something more than mere intake of calories."

Marjorie Kinnan Rawlings,
Cross Creek Cookery

PEPPERS & FETA CHEESE
(See page 145)

Per serving	Low fat	Full fat
Total fat (g)	14	64
Calories	836	1282

MUSHROOM & PESTO
(See page 145)

Per serving	Low fat	Full fat
Total fat (g)	42	116
Calories	1116	1790

For ultimate pizza pizzazz generously mix your favourite ingredients using tantalizing textures, flavours and colours

SAUSAGE & CREAMY
SPINACH *(See page 145)*

Per serving	Low fat	Full fat
Total fat (g)	36	178
Calories	1090	2370

TOMATO & RED ONION
(See page 145)

Per serving	Low fat	Full fat
Total fat (g)	18	88
Calories	830	1530

LAYERED DESSERTS

Opposite:
FRUIT
CREPES
(See page 121)

Per serving	Low fat	Full fat
Total fat (g)	neg	13
Calories	255	325

TAKE NATURE'S GLORIOUS BOUNTY of fruit, add creamy clouds of whipped ricotta, perhaps a dusting of cocoa or a splash or two of intensely fragrant liqueurs, and you have a delicious selection of outrageously rich yet low-fat desserts. They are guaranteed to tempt the taste buds and do no damage to the waistline.

"There is something skewed about an eating regime designed ... for every part of your body except the tip of your tongue."

Ellen Goodman,
Boston Globe

MERINGUE STACK
(See page 135)

Per serving	Low fat	Full fat
Total fat (g)	5	40
Calories	184	477

MANGO MILLEFEUILLE
(See page 136)

Per serving	Low fat	Full fat
Total fat (g)	10	36
Calories	508	890

Heavenly light-as-air layers, with fruits and creamy fillings, form seductive desserts for special occasions

CHOCOLATE CREPES
(See page 121)

Per serving	Low fat	Full fat
Total fat (g)	9	77
Calories	366	886

PASTA

Opposite:
OPEN
RAVIOLI
(See page 108)

Per serving	Low fat	Full fat
Total fat (g)	4	45
Calories	358	726

TAKE A GENEROUS AMOUNT OF A RICH SAUCE full of colourful and nutritious vegetables. Add it to your favourite pasta, with a creamy sauce based on low-fat cheeses, if you like. Sprinkle over plenty of chopped fresh herbs. It all adds up to a dazzling collection of highly satisfying and amazingly low-fat meals.

"Italians do not regard food as merely fuel. They regard it as medicine for the soul..."

Barbara Grizzuti Harrison,
Italian Days (1989)

LASAGNE
(See page 111)

Per serving	Low fat	Full fat
Total fat (g)	12	61
Calories	346	834

FARFALLE WITH PEA
PUREE & PEPPERS
(See page 108)

Per serving	Low fat	Full fat
Total fat (g)	4	23
Calories	462	633

CONCHIGLIONI WITH
BROCCOLI PESTO
(See page 111)

Per serving	Low fat	Full fat
Total fat (g)	9	21
Calories	356	461

For perfect pasta partnerships, mix zingy vegetable toppings, creamy sauces and your favourite pasta

SAUCES & SALSAS

Opposite: VEGETABLE & DUCK *(See pages 52, 65 & 90)*

Per serving	Low fat	Full fat
Total fat (g)	5	39
Calories	160	446

SAUCES AND SALSAS, made from a wide selection of vegetables, fruits and herbs, bring low-fat food to vivid, exuberant life. Anyone who thinks that a low-fat lifestyle equals boredom and austerity just hasn't experienced the full potential of this wonderful food. Who could be bored in the face of such glory?

"You will find salsa on Mexican tables at any time. It is ... refreshing served just with tortillas."

Diana Kennedy, *The Cuisines of Mexico (1982)*

SAUSAGE & ROASTED VEGETABLE SALSA
(See pages 65 & 94)

Per serving	Low fat	Full fat
Total fat (g)	5	22
Calories	450	596

MUSHROOMS MADE WILD
(See page 74)

Per serving	Low fat	Full fat
Total fat (g)	2	9
Calories	102	164

CHICKEN WITH SWEET POTATO & LIME
(See page 88)

Per serving	Low fat	Full fat
Total fat (g)	2	19
Calories	207	336

Spilling lavishly from tortilla cones, sauces and salsas delight the senses with colour and fragrance

FISH

Opposite:
TUNA WITH
LEMON AND
GARLIC
(See page 102)

Per serving	Low fat	Full fat
Total fat (g)	7	71
Calories	265	835

FISH IS THE ULTIMATE HEALTH FOOD, and the ultimate fast food as well. And it is surely the most elegant of ingredients. Cook it quickly, sauce it wisely, and serve with pride. Overcooking, and adding sauces that swamp rather than complement the delicate flavour of the fish, would ruin the whole effect.

*"Fish dinners will make
a man spring
like a flea."*

Thomas Jordan,
(1640)

SALMON WITH YELLOW PEPPER & TARRAGON SAUCE
(See page 104)

Per serving	Low fat	Full fat
Total fat (g)	20	61
Calories	505	873

HALIBUT WITH TOMATO & AUBERGINE
(See page 104)

Per serving	Low fat	Full fat
Total fat (g)	6	53
Calories	378	802

ROASTED MONKFISH WITH GARLIC SAUCE
(See page 103)

Per serving	Low fat	Full fat
Total fat (g)	2	44
Calories	156	536

Why long for Béarnaise? Puréed yellow peppers and a tarragon infusion impart similar luxury to succulent salmon

CREAMY DESSERTS

Opposite:
FRUIT
RICOTTA
TIRAMISU
(See page 127)

Per serving	Low fat	Full fat
Total fat (g)	12	45
Calories	344	651

A LOVELY, LIGHT SOFTNESS characterizes low-fat replacements for cream, such as ricotta, Quark and fromage frais, ensuring that desserts made with them are luxuriously smooth, but never cloying. Intensely fruity conserves, citrus-sharp marmalades and richly dark cocoa powder provide depth of flavour.

"A...hostess excited a solemn children's party to ecstasy by the...words 'Now, let's start with the strawberries and cream'."

Molly Keane,
Nursery Cooking (1985)

Light-as-air mousses and rich, creamy desserts make delicious finales to any meal

BLUEBERRY COMPOTE WITH CREAM TOPPING
(See pages 130 & 137)

Per serving	Low fat	Full fat
Total fat (g)	7	45
Calories	191	480

CHOCOLATE CHEESECAKE MOUSSE
(See page 122)

Per serving	Low fat	Full fat
Total fat (g)	12	60
Calories	277	697

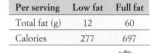

PEACH COMPOTE WITH CREAM TOPPING
(See pages 130 & 137)

Per serving	Low fat	Full fat
Total fat (g)	7	45
Calories	232	519

POULTRY

Opposite: DUCK
BREAST &
CRANBERRY
CHUTNEY
(See page 89)

Per serving	Low fat	Full fat
Total fat (g)	6	62
Calories	241	700

TAKE TONGUE-TINGLING MARINADES, the choice of the glorious spices of Asia and the pick of the world's marvellous production of fruits, vegetables and herbs. Add them to delicately flavoured chicken and more robust duck. The result is an unrivalled selection of low-fat poultry dishes for memorable feasting.

"There is no way of preparing a chicken which I don't like."

Marcella Hazan,
Marcella's Kitchen (1987)

CHICKEN WITH SWEET
POTATO & LIME
(See page 88)

Per serving	Low fat	Full fat
Total fat (g)	2	34
Calories	260	519

CHICKEN BREAST WITH
BRAISED PRUNES
(See page 87)

Per serving	Low fat	Full fat
Total fat (g)	2	40
Calories	178	500

CHICKEN TANDOORI
(See page 86)

Per serving	Low fat	Full fat
Total fat (g)	3	9
Calories	170	239

Zesty marinades; vegetables, herbs and fruits; imaginative seasonings. Use lavishly with poultry for fine flavours

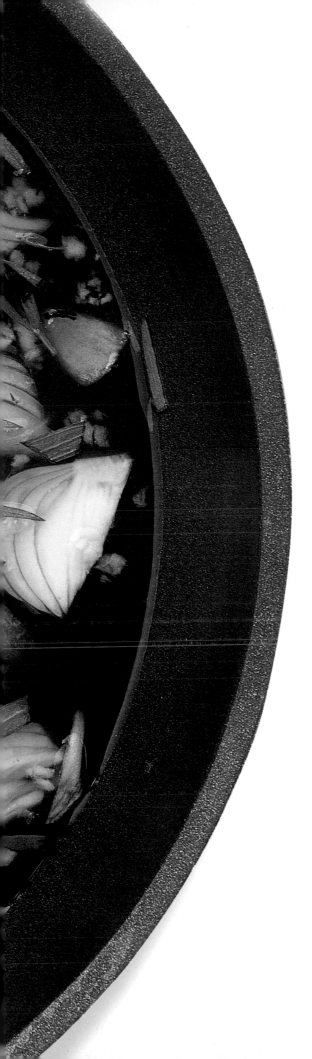

Low Fat Essentials

Successful low-fat cooking depends on good, fresh ingredients carefully prepared and cleverly used and combined with no added fats or very high-fat foods. This section describes food preparation and other techniques that drastically reduce the fat needed in cooking while ensuring that flavour remains high. There are also detailed notes on the wide range of ingredients available to the low-fat cook, and a survey of the kinds of pans, cookware and utensils that help make low-fat cooking easy and enjoyable.

TECHNIQUES

TRADITIONAL CUISINES ARE BASED ON FAT because, for centuries, people needed a great deal of fat for survival. Fat, calorie-dense foods were vital for warmth, energy and for making stored fat for lean times ahead. Today, technology and an ample food supply have drastically decreased our need for fat calories, yet the culinary arts and sciences have stayed in the past. Recipes still insist on the need to sauté in butter, fry in oils, lard and bard with animal fat, enrich with cream and cover with high-fat cheeses.

I believe that it is not enough simply to cut back on fat. To cook our way into the next century, we need to adopt a whole new set of techniques. We will never eliminate fat altogether, nor should we try: we need a small quantity of essential fatty acids each day, and we need the fat-soluble vitamins found in fatty substances. A good variety of vegetables, fruits, whole grains, fish, lean meat and poultry, plus occasional vitamin-fortified foods (cereals and skimmed milk powder, for instance) supply the body's needs.

On the following pages I tell you about the techniques I have developed for taking cooking into a new, low-fat age. First, are techniques to reduce drastically the amount of fat in foodstuffs and recipes. These include oil-water sprays; using stock-sautés instead of the oil, butter and other fats of basic sautéing; and replacing sauces and toppings based on a butter and flour roux, eggs and milk or cream with sauces based on low-fat and no-fat dairy products, vegetable purées and concentrated fat-free stocks. And there is the practical matter of cutting all visible fat off meats and removing all the skin and fat from poultry.

Second, come ways of adding intensified flavour to dishes without fat. Here, my flavour infusion techniques are essential.

Third are techniques based on using vegetables, particularly peppers, garlic and aubergines, as replacements for a proportion of the higher-fat ingredients in dishes and for adding texture, colour and flavour. Finally, we need to be technologically savvy, taking advantage of all the research that has gone into the production of non-stick cooking utensils.

OIL-WATER SPRAYS
see page 29

FLAVOUR INFUSIONS
see pages 32–3

LOW-FAT INGREDIENTS
see pages 40–3

COOKING EQUIPMENT
see pages 38–9

REDUCING FAT IN COOKING

THE SECRETS OF DELICIOUS, rich-tasting, low-fat cooking lie in this handful of basic trustworthy techniques. They allow you to keep fat down and flavour up. The oil-water spray is particularly handy: it delivers far less oil than commercial oil sprays, and the quality of oil – since you choose it yourself – is high. A spritz of olive, safflower or sunflower oil is perfect for roasting or grilling, or try walnut or sesame oil with salads and oriental dishes. The stock sauté paired with a flavour infusion forms another extremely useful technique. Apply these tricks to all your cooking, not just the recipes here.

OIL-WATER SPRAY

For low-fat cooking, frying, even shallow-frying, is out. An oil-water spray allows successful grill-frying or oven-frying. Fill a new, clean plant mister or small plastic spray bottle with seven-eighths water and one-eighth oil. Give the bottle a good shake before using it to spray food or cooking grills, pots and pans. Keep separate bottles for olive oil (for a richer flavour), sunflower oil (for all-purpose use), walnut oil (for a lovely fragrance) and sesame oil (to garnish oriental dishes).

OIL-WATER SPRAY   OLIVE OIL   SUNFLOWER OIL   WALNUT OIL   SESAME OIL

USING THE OIL-WATER SPRAY

1 A light spritz with the oil-water spray gives a sufficient coating on grills and grill pans to allow you to grill and grill-fry fish, meat cutlets and chicken pieces with great success. For oven-frying, use a sturdy, non-stick baking sheet.

2 An oil-water spray allows food for grilling, grill-frying or oven-frying to be given the lightest possible coating of oil, to stop the food drying out or sticking to the pan or baking sheet; brushing oil on food before grilling becomes a thing of the past.

BASIC SAUTEING WITHOUT FATS

Without butter, oil, margarine, how does one manage the basic sauté that begins most savoury recipes? Simple: substitute stock or stock and wine for the fat or oil. Make your own fat-free stock (chicken, vegetable or fish, depending on the recipe), eliminating any initial oil sautéing of conventional stock-making, or buy pots of concentrated stocks now sold by many supermarkets. Mushroom soaking liquid makes a flavour-rich stock (see right). Fresh mushrooms sautéed in stock, wine and Teriyaki sauce rather than oil (120 calories per tablespoon!) have a superb and intense flavour. Another good source of very low-fat stock is Swiss bouillon powder, available in health food stores. Do not use stock cubes, which have a high fat content and which tend to be salty.

MUSHROOM SOAKING LIQUID is a superb stock. Soak dried mushrooms (such as porcini) in plenty of very hot water for 30 minutes. Strain to remove grit. Use both rehydrated mushrooms and the liquid in cooking. Freeze extra stock for later use.

VEGETABLE, CHICKEN AND FISH STOCK can be made without any initial sautéing in oil. The first two can be used in most recipes here; keep fish stock for fish recipes. Strain chicken stock well and chill for several hours before scraping off all fat.

SAUTEING DELICATE FOODS like prawns without fat is easy and flavourful when stock and wine, citrus juice or aromatic sauces replace oil. Flavour infusion ingredients intensify the whole dish. The Cajun Prawns (*left*, and see page 100) are cooked in a flavour infusion reduced twice to intensify the flavour: vegetable or chicken stock, lemon juice and Worcestershire sauce are used for the first reduction; fish stock is poured in for the second reduction.

Two stocks, lemon juice and an aromatic sauce are the liquids in this flavour infusion.

LOW-FAT SAUCES & TOPPINGS

White sauces made with a butter and flour roux (or oil and flour in some parts of the world) and whole milk and/or cream have no place in a modern low-fat lifestyle. Butter–egg yolk emulsion sauces are passé as well, along with beurre blanc and sauces that call for the boiling down of gallons of cream. But wonderful full-bodied sauces can be made with vegetable purées: tomatoes, peppers, aubergines, roasted or braised garlic, even peas. Creamy sauces are also possible given the wealth of no fat, low-fat and medium-fat dairy products available. Particularly successful as a rich topping is a custard of ricotta, egg whites and Parmesan (*below*).

Grilled Vegetable Lasagne (see page 110) with a rich, creamy, yet very low-fat topping.

1 To make the low-fat topping, Ricotta Parmesan Custard (see page 80), first beat egg whites and ricotta cheese together.

2 Add skimmed milk and grated Parmesan for a rich, creamy topping for lasagnes, gratins and similar dishes.

STABILIZING YOGURT

Very low-fat yogurt is thin and watery, and curdles (separates) if you try to cook with it. Make it thick and creamy by straining it in a muslin-lined sieve. Stabilize it for savoury cooking by whisking in Dijon mustard (about a teaspoonful to 300g/10oz) before adding it to a dish during cooking.

REMOVING FAT FROM MEAT & POULTRY

I believe that the occasional serving of lean meat is an important component of a well-rounded diet. Remember that even the leanest cuts of meat, although they may have relatively sparse fat marbling, have surrounding fat that must be trimmed away. Pork tenderloin and pork loin steaks are real standbys, ideal for roasting, pan-braising and grilling, even for mincing for lean sausages (augmented with roasted aubergine – see page 37). Trim the meat well first, with scissors or a sharp knife. Poultry should be trimmed very well, too. In most cases, the fat-laden skin strips away easily, leaving just scraps of skin and fat to be trimmed off.

PORK CHOPS are easily trimmed of their rim of fat, especially if you use kitchen scissors, which are easier and more efficient for the job than a sharp knife.

CHICKEN BREASTS are also easily skinned – simply get a good grip on one edge of the skin and pull, then use scissors or a knife to trim off all traces of skin and fat.

FLAVOUR INFUSIONS

FLAVOUR INFUSIONS MADE BY COOKING DOWN good stock and wine with a selection of well-chosen flavour components replace the oil- and butter-based sautés of conventional cooking. The infusion ensures that the finished dish resonates with round, intense and well-balanced flavour. As in most conventional sautés, a flavour infusion for low-fat cooking begins with onions and garlic, then other ingredients are added, according to the nature of the particular recipe. Illustrated on this page are the main groups of ingredients that are used in various combinations to give flavour infusions their individual intensity.

BASIC INGREDIENTS

These groups are not definitive: cook's preferences and what is in the kitchen cupboard will suggest alternatives.

SPICES *(below) give flavour and colour to infusions. When simmered in stock and wine, they become gentle and mellow, and all their flavour is released to mingle with other tastes.*

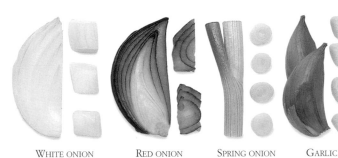

WHITE ONION   RED ONION   SPRING ONION   GARLIC

ONIONS AND GARLIC
(left) are basics, though the garlic could be omitted. Red onions are used for extra colour density and flavour.
BLACK OLIVES *(below) add all the unique flavour of olive oil for a fraction of the calories.*

PAPRIKA   TURMERIC

CUMIN   CORIANDER

CHILLIES, *fresh or dried, add zest. The hotter the chillies, the hotter the infusion. Deseeding and ribbing reduces their heat.*
SUN-DRIED TOMATOES *add a caramelized smokiness. Choose dry-packed varieties.*

RED CHILLIES   GREEN CHILLIES   CHILLI FLAKES   SUN-DRIED TOMATOES   BLACK OLIVES

CARROT   FENNEL   PEPPERS   CELERY

VEGETABLES *contribute taste, texture and splendid nutrition. Among the most frequently used in flavour infusions are carrots, fennel, peppers (red, yellow or orange for a sweeter flavour) and celery.*

BASIC LIQUIDS *of flavour infusions are good quality stocks (chicken, vegetable or fish, depending on the recipe) and wines (red, white, vermouth or sherry). Drizzles of aromatic and intense liquids such as vinegars and spicy sauces can be added for even deeper flavour.*

STOCK   RED WINE   BALSAMIC VINEGAR   TERIYAKI SAUCE   WORCESTERSHIRE SAUCE

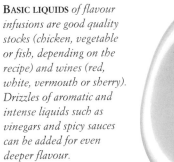

MAKING A FLAVOUR INFUSION

For a basic flavour infusion, as in Tomato Sauce (see page 66), the ingredients are simmered, covered first to "gentle" the onions, then uncovered to reduce the liquid.

TOMATO SAUCE INFUSION INGREDIENTS

2 red onions, chopped

4 sun-dried tomatoes, chopped

4 black olives, slivered off their stones

pinch or two of dried chilli flakes

4 garlic cloves

175ml (6fl oz) stock

175ml (6fl oz) red wine

1 Simmer these ingredients briskly until tender and the liquid has almost gone. This intensely concentrates the flavour.

2 Add the remaining Tomato Sauce ingredients, except the herbs, in stages to the infusion and simmer to a thick sauce.

3 If the sauce is to be used at once, add the herbs. If the sauce is to be frozen, omit the herbs until it is to be used.

SIMMERING THE FLAVOUR INFUSION ingredients uncovered (*above*) concentrates the flavour before the remaining Tomato Sauce ingredients are added (*left*). Plenty of fresh herbs give the finished sauce freshness and even more crisp flavour.

OTHER WAYS OF PREPARING FLAVOUR INFUSIONS

STIR-FRYING: with this method, as in Cauliflower Stir-fried in Red Wine (see page 69), the flavour infusion ingredients are initially stir-fried very quickly. They reach tenderness in the final stages.

BRAISING: as in Chicken Breasts with Braised Prunes & Shallots (see page 87), the flavour infusion ingredients are braised in the pan in which the main ingredients have already been browned.

SAUTEING: this method involves using the flavour infusion ingredients in a sauté, as in Cajun Prawns (see page 100). In this case, the infusion is still quite liquid when the prawns are added.

PEPPERS & GARLIC

PEPPERS AND GARLIC are both endlessly useful in low-fat cooking, creating rich, round flavour without adding fat. Stunningly attractive red and yellow peppers (green ones lack sweetness) make food beautiful and delicious, and they add valuable nutrients as well. Grilled and skinned, or peeled raw and then simmered or sautéed, or infused and sieved, they are exquisitely sweet and digestible. Garlic, especially when roasted or braised, adds texture and profound depths to soups, stews and sauces.

SAUTEING PEPPERS

1 To prepare red or yellow peppers for sautéing, first cut them in half and remove the stems, ribs and seeds. Cut the halves into their natural sections.

2 Using a swivel-bladed vegetable peeler, which removes vegetable skins very thinly and thus saves valuable nutrients (*left*), peel the skin off the pepper sections. Without its skin, pepper flesh cooks to melting, sweet and digestible tenderness.

3 For sautéing, dice the peeled pepper sections or cut them into strips, as in Silky Stir-fried Pepper Strips, (*below*; see page 71 for recipe), and sauté in hot stock. Gentle stirring with wooden spoons ensures the pepper pieces do not break up as they cook.

A well-flavoured stock replaces fat or oil as the medium for low-fat sautéing.

INFUSING PEPPERS

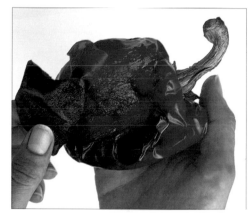

1 For sauces, e.g. Pepper Sauce (see page 64), simmer unpeeled pepper pieces in an infusion until soft. Pour into a blender.

2 Purée the peppers and the greatly reduced infusion in the blender into a thick sauce.

3 To remove the indigestible pepper skins, push the sauce through a sieve.

GRILLING PEPPERS

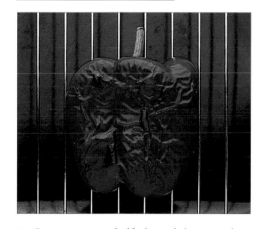

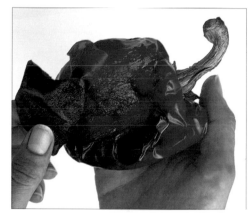

1 Cut peppers in half, deseed them, and flatten the pieces slightly. Grill under a hot grill until charred and blackened.

2 Put the hot pepper halves in a covered bowl or plastic bag for a few minutes. This makes the skins easier to remove.

3 Strip off the blackened skins. Use the wonderfully smoky flavoured peppers as they are or as a cooking ingredient.

PREPARING GARLIC

TO ROAST GARLIC, take a whole, firm, non-sprouting head of garlic and remove its papery outer covering. Do not separate the cloves. Slice off the pointed end. Wrap the whole head of garlic in foil, shiny side in, and roast in an oven preheated to 190°C/375°F/gas 5, until the garlic turns into a purée (about 45 minutes). Cool the head of garlic (*left*), then separate the cloves and squeeze out the purée. Use the purée in recipes calling for garlic, or simply – and unforgettably – as a spread for fresh, crusty bread.

CRUSH GARLIC with a wooden mallet. Hit separated cloves lightly to loosen the skins. Remove skins, then beat cloves to a pulp.

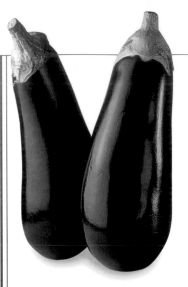

AUBERGINES

WITHOUT THIS GLORIOUS, GLOSSY PURPLE VEGETABLE low-fat cooking would be much less interesting. Aubergine flesh makes the leanest of minced meat – usually dry, juiceless and unrewarding when cooked – juicy and succulent, and it stretches meat so that a small amount goes a long way. It does these things directly, deliciously, with no conflicting flavour or off-putting texture. The overall impression of a meat dish with aubergine included will be lighter, but not at all insubstantial.

USING RAW AUBERGINES

1 Use a swivel-bladed vegetable peeler to remove the skin from the aubergine as thinly as possible.

2 Trim the peeled aubergine and use a long-bladed knife to cut it lengthways into slices about 1cm (½in) thick.

3 Cut the slices across into evenly shaped cubes. The aubergine flesh is now ready for using in flavour infusions.

4 Cubes of aubergine are the main ingredient in the flavour infusion for Bolognese Sauce (*left*, and see page 62). Cooked in an infusion, the aubergine flesh becomes meltingly tender, and the cubes soak up the flavours like little sponges.

Cubes of aubergine cook gently among the flavour infusion ingredients for Bolognese Sauce.

ROASTING AUBERGINES

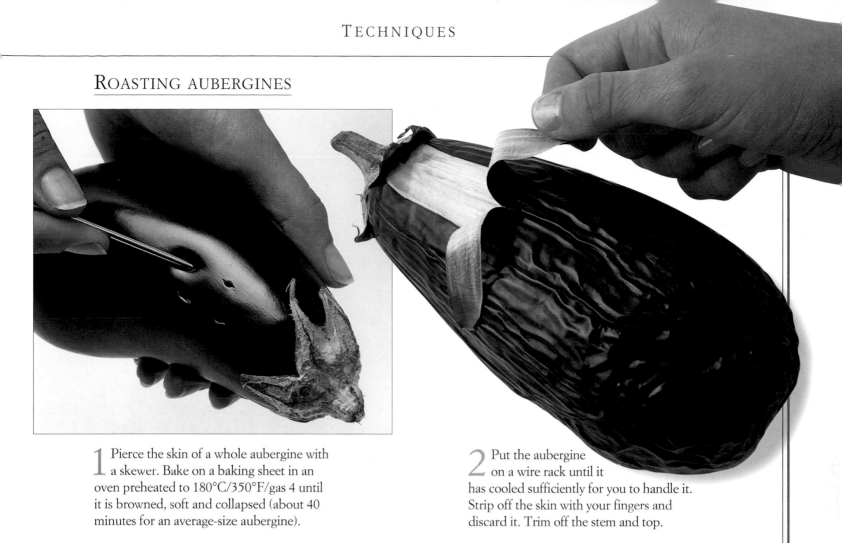

1 Pierce the skin of a whole aubergine with a skewer. Bake on a baking sheet in an oven preheated to 180°C/350°F/gas 4 until it is browned, soft and collapsed (about 40 minutes for an average-size aubergine).

2 Put the aubergine on a wire rack until it has cooled sufficiently for you to handle it. Strip off the skin with your fingers and discard it. Trim off the stem and top.

3 Cut the aubergine, first into slices lengthways, then across into cubes. Because it is so soft, the aubergine flesh quickly becomes a rough purée. If you prefer, purée it briefly in a food processor or blender. (Don't over-purée it.)

4 The roasted aubergine purée is now ready to be added, as a meat extender, to recipes like Spicy, Citrus-scented Mexican Sausages (see page 94) or (*as above*) to Piquant Lemon Herb Meatballs (see page 95).

EQUIPMENT

MODERN, HEAVY-BASED, NON-STICK cookware makes low-fat cooking easier and more efficient than it used to be. The recipes in this book use a wide selection of non-stick pans along with a few well-chosen machines. A blender, for instance, is perfect for making vegetable purée sauces, and a food processor quickly makes pâtés, dips and dessert toppings. Add to these a good assortment of the usual kitchen standbys, including whisks, bowls, measuring utensils and top quality tools, and cooking becomes a great pleasure.

SWISS ROLL TIN, *or baking tray (left), is non-stick and ideal for baking Chocolate Roulade (see page 118) or the sheet cake for Cassata (see page 143).*

LOAF TIN *(left), also non-stick, is ideal for baking tea breads.*

FLAN TIN *with a removable base (left) is useful for baking clafoutis, whether sweet or savoury.*

CAKE TIN *(right), with a non-stick finish, is used to bake several recipes in this book.*

MUFFIN TIN *(left), for perfectly baked Spoonbread Corn Muffins (see page 154).*

BAKING PARCHMENT *(below, left), also called silicone paper, requires no greasing before biscuits or meringues are spooned or piped on to it.*

BAKING SHEET *with a non-stick coating (below) has a wide variety of uses, from roasting aubergines to baking biscuits.*

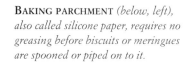

ANGEL FOOD CAKE TIN *(above) is a must for baking Angel Cake (see page 143).*

KITCHEN GADGETS

Well-chosen kitchen machines, with
such basics as sieves, wooden spoons,
kitchen knives, measuring jugs and
spoons, scales and a range of
glass bowls and baking
dishes make low-fat
cooking efficient.

SIEVE

WOODEN
SPOON

GLASS BOWL   PLASTIC SPRAY BOTTLE   FOOD PROCESSOR

BLENDER

BLENDER, *also called a liquidizer, is
ideal for processing soups and sauces
to exactly the right consistency.*

OIL-WATER SPRAY, *an essential of
low-fat cooking, is easily and
inexpensively made in a plastic spray
bottle; look for clean, new, plant
misters or scent spray bottles.*

FOOD PROCESSOR *mixes dry
ingredients, chops vegetables and fruits,
whips up purées, pâtés and dips, and
makes instant ice creams and sorbets.*

WOODEN MALLET (*or the wooden end of a steak
tenderizing mallet) is ideal for loosening the skin
of a garlic clove, and then crushing it to a pulp.*

VEGETABLE PEELER *with a
swivel blade peels skin off
vegetables very thinly,
wasting as little as possible
of the flesh beneath.*

CAKE TESTER *tests cakes,
of course, and doubles as
a skewer for piercing
vegetables such as
aubergines and potatoes
before baking.*

NON-STICK WOK AND STEAMER: *use the wok for
no-fat stir-frying and sautéing, and the combination
of wok and steamer for steaming and smoking.
Choose a wok with a tight-fitting lid.*

FRYING PAN *with a non-
stick surface allows foods
to be sautéed in stock
and wine rather than
in fats or oils.
A pan with a
diameter of
30cm (12in)
is a good, all-
purpose size.*

OMELETTE PAN *with a
non-stick surface allows
omelettes and other dishes
to cook very quickly with
no need to grease the pan.*

GRILL PAN *with non-stick
ridges grills meat, poultry
and vegetables on the hob. It
imparts a smoky, barbecue
flavour, and characteristic
hatchmarks.*

INGREDIENTS

THE EXCITEMENT OF THIS SPECIAL KIND of cooking lies in the lack of added fats and oils and high-fat dairy products, not only for the obvious health benefits, but for the fresh vibrancy and depth of flavour that results from their absence. A surfeit of fatty, greasy ingredients is cloying; it clogs the tastebuds and muddles the balance of flavours. Without the glut of fat, the panoply of fresh and natural ingredients that forms the basis of this cuisine shines through in all its glory. Certain ingredients are used repeatedly; they are as important to the basic techniques of this cuisine as butter, oil, animal fats and cream are to traditional cuisines.

VEGETABLES

Vegetables are vital to the techniques of this low-fat cuisine; they add colour, nutrition, texture, bulk and flavour. Nutritionally and sensually, they are the main reason why this discipline works so well and the food is so satisfying.

GARLIC, *mellow and melting, roasted or pan-braised, adds texture and complexity. It is also used crushed and stock-sautéed.*

CHILLIES *come in all sizes and degrees of heat. Often, smaller means hotter. Remove seeds and ribs for less heat. Dried chilli flakes are useful.*

CANNED BEANS *come in many varieties (above are borlotti beans), and save the long soaking and simmering dried beans need.*

PASSATA *is sieved tomato; not as thick or intense as tomato purée.*

BLACK OLIVES *in brine, bottled or vacuum-packed, are slivered off their stones and used in infusions for a fraction of the fat of olive oil.*

AUBERGINE *is a magic ingredient. Roast, peel and purée, then use to stretch extra-lean mince and make it succulent, or chop and use in an infusion. It will resonate with flavour.*

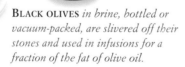

TOMATO PUREE *used in small quantities adds deep colour and intense tomato flavour.*

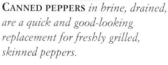

DRIED MUSHROOMS *(porcini) soaked in warm water make a powerful wild mushroom stock for flavour infusions. Strain to remove grit.*

CANNED PEPPERS *in brine, drained, are a quick and good-looking replacement for freshly grilled, skinned peppers.*

PEPPERS *are endlessly useful, either raw and peeled for sautés and infusions, or grilled and skinned for smoky purées and sauces.*

CANNED TOMATOES, *whole or chopped, are used in sauces, soups, casseroles and stews.*

SUN-DRIED TOMATOES, *dry-packed, snipped into an infusion, give a deep, smoky, caramelized taste.*

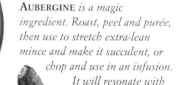

SAUCES

Several bottled sauces are invaluable shortcuts to building complex flavour. They can be used as seasoning, in infusions or in marinades, always in small amounts so that they do not overpower other ingredients in the recipe.

HOISIN SAUCE *is often referred to as "Chinese barbecue sauce".*

WORCESTERSHIRE SAUCE *is unique and anchovy-spiked. It pairs well with Tabasco.*

TABASCO SAUCE, *made with peppers, is piquant and zippy, for fans of edible fire.*

TERIYAKI SAUCE *adds depth. If you cannot find it, use soy sauce.*

OILS & VINEGARS

Oils, in tiny amounts in the oil-water spray, are used for seasoning, for lubrication and to prevent sticking. Vinegars add a tang to low-fat dishes.

OLIVE OIL *has incomparable flavour. Use the best extra-virgin olive oil.*

SUNFLOWER OIL *is used when a neutral flavour is needed.*

SESAME OIL *flavours oriental dishes. As always, only a spritz is needed.*

SAFFLOWER OIL, *like sunflower oil, is used for a neutral taste.*

BALSAMIC VINEGAR *is treacly, rich, sweet-and-sour nectar.*

OLIVE OIL.   SUNFLOWER OIL   SESAME OIL   SAFFLOWER OIL   BALSAMIC VINEGAR

HERBS

Nothing compares with the pungent intensity of fresh herbs. Mix and match to taste.

BASIL *has a spicy flavour, with hints of clove and pepper. It is delicious with garlic, lemon and tomatoes.*

CORIANDER *has an unusual, almost musty taste. Once you get used to it, you'll adore it.*

FLAT-LEAF PARSLEY *has more flavour than the curly variety.*

ROSEMARY *has pungent needles, to be cooked rather than used as a garnish.*

MINT *is splendid in savoury recipes as well as sweet, and epitomizes freshness.*

SPICES

Mixtures of ground spices, simmered in an infusion with other ingredients, give a well-rounded flavour.

DIJON MUSTARDS *and flavoured mustards add an interesting dimension to recipes, and stabilize low-fat yogurt.*

TURMERIC *has lovely colour and a bracing freshness.*

PAPRIKA *varies in taste from mildly hot to mild and sweet.*

CHILLI POWDER *(cayenne) is pure ground chillies and should be used with care.*

CORIANDER SEEDS, *ground, have a different taste from the fresh leaves.*

FRESH ROOT GINGER *should be sliced, peeled and crushed with a wooden mallet.*

DAIRY PRODUCTS

There are superb medium-fat and skimmed milk dairy products available, providing rich creaminess without the heavy cloying effect of full-fat products. Use in sauces, dips, and – most exciting – desserts. Since many of the products they replace are 80 per cent fat, the dairy products here are to be cherished.

QUARK *is smooth, creamy and skimmed (0% fat), slightly tangy but not sour, and wonderful in all sorts of recipes.*

RICOTTA *is sweet and creamy, 14% fat, and a perfect substitute for much higher fat crème fraîche, whipped cream and mascarpone.*

MOZZARELLA *(half-fat version is 10% fat) comes in liquid-filled pouches and melts beautifully. It is mild and milky.*

SKIMMED MILK POWDER *is fortified with fat-soluble vitamins A and D. Add it to skimmed milk for extra body, richness and nutrition.*

SKIMMED MILK *seems richer when it is mixed with skimmed milk powder. Use it in soups and sauces and for luscious puddings.*

VERY LOW-FAT YOGURT *can be drained in a muslin-lined sieve; it will be as thick as the higher fat Greek kind.*

FROMAGE FRAIS *is made from cultured skimmed milk. Thick, creamy and slightly tangy, it replaces sour cream, crème fraîche and cream.*

WINES

Red and white wines and fortified wines combine with stock to form the basic sauté liquid that replaces butter and oils. In simmering, the alcohol evaporates, but full-bodied flavour remains. Small amounts of various liqueurs give fragrance to desserts.

RED WINE *should be a decent, drinkable dry red, not too expensive.*

WHITE WINE *should, ideally, be a dry one for a lighter effect.*

AMARETTO *has a delicate almond fragrance, excellent in desserts.*

SHERRY *is perfect in mushroom sautés and sauces and bean soups.*

COINTREAU *mixed with orange juice and vanilla is exquisite in desserts.*

VERMOUTH, *with its herby bouquet, is a fabulous cooking ingredient.*

RED WINE

WHITE WINE

AMARETTO

SHERRY

VERMOUTH

COINTREAU

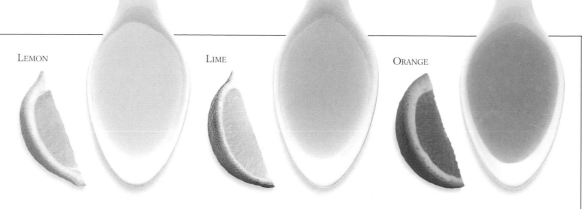

JUICES

Citrus juices are important for their tenderizing properties, and the spark that their acid edge brings. Grated citrus zest (the skin without the underlying bitter white pith) is important as well.

LEMON

LIME

ORANGE

DESSERTS

Rich-tasting low-fat desserts are possible when you use the full range of low-fat dairy products, and add other well chosen goodies: low-fat cocoa powder, the best high-cocoa-solid chocolate, fragrant liqueurs, perfectly ripe fruit, conserves, preserves.... I like old-fashioned desserts brought up-to-date with a fresher, lighter profile. Bread puddings, rice puddings, crumbles, clafoutis, even Tiramisù will take on a new, more modern character.

PLAIN CHOCOLATE *to choose is one with at least 70% cocoa solids.*

COCOA POWDER *should be low-fat; it is intensely chocolatey.*

CORNFLOUR *is sometimes used in small amounts to thicken sauces.*

GRAPE NUTS *cereal crushed with Amaretti make a splendid crumb crust.*

AMARETTI BISCUITS *to choose are those flavoured with apricot kernels, rather than high-fat almonds.*

DRIED PEARS *make a delicious addition to dried fruit compotes.*

DRIED PEACHES *can be used in compotes, puddings, conserves and in baking.*

DRIED APRICOTS *are almost more palatable than the fresh fruit and are good in desserts and baking.*

DRIED FIGS *are another excellent dried fruit. Eat them as they are or use in desserts and baking.*

DRIED CHERRIES, *along with raisins, sultanas, dried blueberries and cranberries, are dessert basics.*

VANILLA
EXTRACT

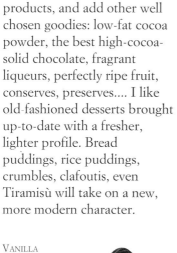

VANILLA *in pod and extract (not the harsh essence) form is much used. Scrape the seeds from the pod and use as seasoning; reuse the pod.*

VANILLA
POD

CONSERVES *are often used in place of sugar for a more interesting balance of flavour.*

MARMALADE *is another delicious sweetener that can be used instead of sugar.*

HONEY *can be whisked into fromage frais for a gorgeous, creamy topping.*

FILO PASTRY *has delicate layers that can be coated with purchased oil spray instead of the traditional butter.*

APRICOT

BLUEBERRY

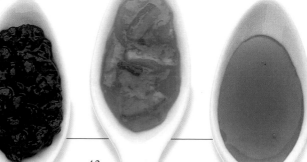

43

RECIPES

HERE IS LOW-FAT COOKING TO CHERISH: MORE

THAN 150 RECIPES IN WHICH A WIDE-RANGING CHOICE OF

THE WORLD'S FINEST INGREDIENTS ARE LAVISHED ON AN

EXHILARATING ARRAY OF DISHES DESIGNED TO DELIGHT THE

TASTE BUDS AND SATISFY EVERY APPETITE. RECIPES

FOR SALADS, SNACKS AND STARTERS PROVIDE OPPORTUNITIES

FOR GUILT-FREE SNACKING BETWEEN MEALS. THERE

IS A SPLENDID RANGE OF MAIN COURSE DISHES, USING MEAT,

POULTRY, FISH, VEGETABLES, PASTA AND GRAINS, AND A

MOUTHWATERING COLLECTION OF DESSERTS AND BAKING,

INCLUDING BREADS, CAKES AND BISCUITS.

SOUPS & STARTERS

AN ARRAY OF CROSTINI, served with a selection of dips and spreads, is an inspiring way to begin a meal for those who love lots of colour and texture. Soup is also a marvellous way to get things going. With a variety of vegetables, spices, herbs and flavour infusions, building complex layers of flavour into soup is one of the most satisfying of kitchen activities; I put it right up there with bread making. In fact, crostini and soup are such perfect companions, and such a feast of good nutrition, that the meal need go no further.

FRAGRANT VEGETABLE SOUP

Another name for this recipe could be "new wave minestrone" – it is as good a way as any to describe this gently spiced, lime-spiked combination of vegetables, herbs and tiny pasta shapes.

INGREDIENTS

1 red onion, roughly chopped

1 carrot, halved lengthways, then cut across into chunks

1 yellow and 1 red pepper, ribbed, deseeded, peeled and chopped (see page 34)

1 red chilli, deseeded and finely chopped

juice of 1 lime

grated zest of ¼ lime

1 tsp ground cumin

½ tsp ground paprika

1.8 litres (3 pints) vegetable stock (see page 30)

500g (1lb) potatoes, peeled and cut into 2.5cm (1in) chunks

1 bulb fennel, 500g (1lb), halved and cut into 2.5cm (1in) chunks

425g (14oz) canned tomatoes, well drained and cut into strips

250g (8oz) frozen sweetcorn kernels

2 courgettes, about 180g (6oz) each, halved lengthways and cut across into 2.5cm (1in) slices

1 tbsp tomato purée

juice of ½ large orange

60g (2oz) tiny soup pasta

several dashes of Tabasco sauce, to taste (optional)

salt and freshly ground black pepper

chopped flat-leaf parsley, to garnish

1 Put the onion, carrot, peppers, chilli, half the lime juice and all the zest, spices and 300ml (½ pint) of the stock into a heavy-based saucepan. Cover, bring to the boil, and simmer briskly for 10 minutes.

2 Uncover the pan and add another 150ml (¼ pint) of the stock, the potatoes and the fennel. Simmer briskly for 6–8 minutes, until the liquid is almost gone and the vegetables are half-cooked. Stir in the tomatoes, and season. Stir in 125ml (4fl oz) of the stock, simmer for 4–5 minutes, then stir in the sweetcorn and courgettes. Simmer for 3–4 minutes.

3 Put 3 tablespoons of the soup mixture (excluding potato or courgette pieces) into a blender with the tomato purée and 3–4 tablespoons stock and blend to a smooth purée. Stir back into the soup and bring to a simmer. Add the remaining stock, lime juice, and orange juice. Add the soup pasta, and Tabasco sauce, if using.

4 Simmer for 7–10 minutes, partially covered, until the pasta is tender. Taste, adding salt and pepper and a few drops of lime juice, orange juice or Tabasco, as needed. Stir in the parsley. Serve the soup topped with a spoonful of Grilled Pepper & Oregano Pistou (see page 65), if liked.

Per serving	
Total fat (g)	3
Saturated fat (g)	1
Unsaturated fat (g)	2
Cholesterol (mg)	0
Sodium (mg)	327
Calories	260

Makes
6 servings

FRAGRANT VEGETABLE SOUP
*is a lightly spiced mix of many kinds
of colourful vegetables and tiny
soup pasta shapes.*

RED BEAN, GRILLED PEPPER & AUBERGINE SOUP

A colour-contrasted swirl of yellow pepper purée makes a dramatic garnish to this velvety bowl of soup.

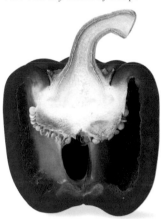

INGREDIENTS

600ml (1 pint) Tomato Aubergine Sauce (page 62)

four 425g (14oz) cans red kidney beans, drained and rinsed

600ml (1 pint) stock (see page 30)

several dashes of Tabasco sauce

several dashes of Worcestershire sauce

salt and freshly ground black pepper

1 red pepper, grilled (see page 35)

1 yellow pepper, grilled (see page 35)

½ tsp Sambal Oelek (hot chilli condiment)

1 Put the sauce, beans and stock in a saucepan and season with the Tabasco and Worcestershire sauces, plus salt and pepper to taste. Simmer for 10 minutes. Leave to cool slightly.

2 Cut the red pepper into pieces and add (with any juices) to the soup. Purée the soup in the liquidizer, in batches, to a velvety smooth texture.

3 Purée the yellow pepper with the Sambal Oelek. Serve the soup in soup plates with a swirl of the yellow pepper purée on top.

 Per serving

Total fat (g)	2
Saturated fat (g)	1
Unsaturated fat (g)	1
Cholesterol (mg)	0
Sodium (mg)	1077
Calories	295

Makes
6 servings

SPICY SWEET POTATO BISQUE

Breathtaking colour, compelling texture and lots of pizzazz make this a soup to cherish. Its creamy texture is amazing when you consider that it contains no cream, indeed no dairy products at all. It is a testimony to the versatility of vegetable purées.

INGREDIENTS

1.5 litres (2½ pints) vegetable stock (see page 30)

juice of 2 limes

2 red onions, chopped

6 large garlic cloves, crushed

one 1cm (½in) piece fresh root ginger, peeled and crushed

4 sun-dried tomatoes, chopped

1–2 pinches dried chilli flakes

½ tsp ground turmeric

1 tsp ground cumin

½ tsp ground coriander

500g (1lb) baking potatoes, peeled and cut into chunks

1kg (2lb) orange-fleshed sweet potatoes, peeled and cut into chunks

several dashes of Tabasco sauce

salt and freshly ground black pepper

chopped fresh chives, to garnish

1 Put 300ml (½ pint) of the stock, the juice of 1 lime, the onions, garlic, ginger, sun-dried tomatoes, chilli flakes and spices in a heavy-based saucepan. Cover and bring to a brisk simmer. Uncover and continue simmering until the liquid has almost gone, and the onions are "frying" in their own juices.

2 Add the potatoes and stir over a moderate heat until they begin to catch a little, and are well coated with the onions, garlic and spices. Stir in the remaining stock and several dashes of Tabasco sauce. Simmer, partially covered, for 15 minutes or so, until the potatoes are very tender.

3 If you have an immersion blender, put it into the pot and purée the soup. Otherwise, cool the soup slightly and purée in batches in an ordinary blender, holding down the cover. The soup should be smooth and velvety. Return the purée to the pan and add the remaining lime juice, and more stock, if it seems too thick. Taste and add salt, pepper and more Tabasco as needed. Serve garnished with chopped chives.

 Per serving

Total fat (g)	1
Saturated fat (g)	<1
Unsaturated fat (g)	<1
Cholesterol (mg)	0
Sodium (mg)	306
Calories	277

 Makes
6 servings

WHITE BEAN, SWEET POTATO & FENNEL SOUP

More a vegetable stew than a soup, this spicy bowlful of goodness would make a great meal with garlic bread. To make a creamy soup, purée the slightly cooled soup in a blender. Return to the pan, add stock to thin it a little, and season.

INGREDIENTS

900ml (1½ pints) stock (see page 30)

125ml (4fl oz) Amontillado sherry

2 fennel bulbs, trimmed and chopped

6 spring onions, trimmed and sliced

1 courgette, about 125g (4oz), trimmed and roughly chopped

1 orange-fleshed sweet potato, peeled and roughly chopped

2 garlic cloves, crushed

5mm (¼in) slice fresh root ginger, peeled and crushed

1 red chilli, deseeded and chopped

1 tsp ground turmeric

1 tsp ground paprika

1½ tsp ground cumin

1½ tsp ground coriander

juice of 1 orange

juice of ½ lime

two 400g (13oz) cans cannellini beans, rinsed and drained

1 yellow pepper, grilled and skinned (see page 35) and diced

salt and freshly ground black pepper

chopped fresh parsley and coriander, to garnish

1 Put 300ml (½ pint) of the stock into a heavy-based saucepan or wok. Add the sherry, fennel, onions, courgette, sweet potato, garlic, ginger, chilli, spices and citrus juices. Cover and boil for 5 minutes. Remove the cover and simmer briskly, until the vegetables are tender and "frying" in their juices.

2 Stir in the beans and pepper, with any juices. Season with salt and pepper, pour in the remaining stock and simmer for 5 minutes. Cool slightly.

3 Ladle 300ml (½ pint) of the soup into a blender and blend until smooth. Stir back into the soup. Bring to a simmer, taste, and adjust the seasonings if necessary. Serve strewn with herbs.

Per serving

Total fat (g)	2
Saturated fat (g)	1
Unsaturated fat (g)	1
Cholesterol (mg)	0
Sodium (mg)	697
Calories	200

Makes
6 servings

BUTTERNUT SQUASH, GINGER & LIME PUREE

This blazingly orange purée is smooth, rich and spicy. Spread it on the best bread as part of a selection of crostini, serve it as a dip, or in little pots at the table, instead of butter.

INGREDIENTS

1 butternut squash

oil-water spray (see page 29)

2 large garlic cloves

2.5cm (1in) piece fresh root ginger, peeled

Amontillado sherry (see method)

salt and freshly ground black pepper

2 tbsp buttermilk or fromage frais

several dashes of Tabasco sauce

several dashes of Worcestershire sauce

juice of ½ lime

1 Halve the squash lengthways and scrape out the seeds and fibre. Oil-water spray the cut side of each half and put, cut side up, on a baking sheet.

2 Crush together the garlic and ginger, and put half the mixture into each squash half. Fill each cavity three-quarters full with sherry. Season each half with salt and plenty of pepper.

3 Roast the squash halves in a preheated oven for 45 minutes, or until the squash flesh is very tender. Several times during the baking, dabble a pastry brush in the cavities, and brush the tops of the squash with the sherry (when the squash is tender, the sherry will have almost evaporated).

4 Remove from the oven and leave to cool, draped with a clean tea towel.

5 Scrape the squash pulp and ginger-garlic mixture into a food processor. Add the remaining ingredients. Process until very smooth. Taste and add more salt, pepper, lime juice, Tabasco or Worcestershire sauce, as needed.

Per recipe quantity

Total fat (g)	2
Saturated fat (g)	<1
Unsaturated fat (g)	1
Cholesterol (mg)	1
Sodium (mg)	70
Calories	268

Oven temperature
200°C/400°F/gas 6

Baking time
45 minutes

Makes
600ml (1 pint)

GREEN PEA GUACAMOLE

I've been substituting peas for avocado to make a fresh and herby low-fat version of guacamole ever since I read Michael Robert's brilliant suggestion in Secret Ingredients. *Use the best brand of bottled salsa you can find in the guacamole, which is illustrated on page 61.*

INGREDIENTS

1–2 large garlic cloves, crushed

1 tbsp lime juice

1 tbsp lemon juice

500g (1lb) frozen petits pois, thawed

2 tbsp chopped parsley

2 tbsp chopped coriander

1 tbsp shredded mint

1–2 tbsp Mexican Salsa (choose medium or hot according to your taste)

salt

1 Put the garlic in a glass bowl or jug. Add the lime and lemon juices and allow to marinate for 10 minutes.

2 Put the garlic mixture, petits pois, herbs and Mexican Salsa into a food processor. Add salt to taste, and process to an almost smooth texture. Taste again, and add more lime juice, Mexican Salsa and salt as needed.

VARIATION

Pea Purée: simmer together 500g (1lb) thawed petits pois, 350ml (12fl oz) stock, 2 lightly crushed garlic cloves and the juice of ½ lime until the peas are cooked but still bright green. Purée the mixture in a blender until velvety smooth. Season with salt and pepper and stir in a tablespoon of torn fresh mint. Add the juice of the leftover half lime, if liked.

Per recipe quantity

Total fat (g)	5
Saturated fat (g)	1
Unsaturated fat (g)	4
Cholesterol (mg)	0
Sodium (mg)	175
Calories	267

Makes
600ml (1 pint),
(about 4 servings)

HOISIN-LEMON RUBY BEETROOT SPREAD

Oven-roasted beetroot, roughly puréed and laced with flavourings that augment and counterpoint their earthiness, make a glowing spread.

INGREDIENTS

250g (8oz) oven-roasted beetroot, cut into chunks (see page 78)

1½ tbsp Hoisin sauce

2 tbsp lemon juice

Put all the ingredients in a food processor and process to a slightly rough purée. Taste, and add a little more Hoisin sauce and lemon juice, to taste.

VARIATION

Replace the Hoisin sauce with a purchased hot mango chutney, added to taste.

 Per recipe quantity

Total fat (g)	1
Saturated fat (g)	neg.
Unsaturated fat (g)	1
Cholesterol (mg)	0
Sodium (mg)	462
Calories	133

Makes
300ml (½ pint)

SWEET POTATO SPREAD

Another smooth, rich and vivid purée to spread on bread, or to use as a dip. The sweet potato takes on a buttery, creamy texture as it cooks, and the spices and citrus juices set off its sweetness perfectly.

INGREDIENTS

1 sweet potato, about 425g (14oz)

2 large garlic cloves, crushed

3 sun-dried tomatoes, chopped

½–1 chilli, deseeded and chopped

½ tbsp turmeric

½ tsp ground cumin

½ tsp ground coriander

½ tsp paprika

juice of ½ lime

2 tbsp lemon juice

300ml (½ pint) stock (see page 30)

1–2 tbsp buttermilk or fromage frais

salt and freshly ground black pepper

1 Pierce the potato in several places with a thin skewer. Bake in a preheated oven, directly on the oven shelf, until tender.

2 Meanwhile, put the remaining ingredients except the buttermilk and salt and pepper in a frying pan, and simmer briskly until the liquid is almost gone.

3 Split the sweet potato and scrape the flesh into a food processor. Add the spice mixture, buttermilk and seasoning. Process to a smooth, buttery purée. Taste and adjust the seasonings and citrus juices as needed.

 Per recipe quantity

Total fat (g)	4
Saturated fat (g)	1
Unsaturated fat (g)	3
Cholesterol (mg)	<1
Sodium (mg)	473
Calories	467

Oven temperature:
200°C/400°F/gas 6

Baking time
about 45 minutes

Makes
250ml (8fl oz)

WILD MUSHROOM PATE

This is a deep, dark pâté. It is splendid spread on the best crusty bread you can find, either as part of a selection of crostini or on its own.

INGREDIENTS

1 quantity Mushrooms Made Wild (see page 74)

1 tsp red pepper Dijon mustard

few drops lemon juice

Put all the ingredients in the bowl of a food processor and process to a dark, rough purée, adding more lemon juice to taste.

 Per serving

Total fat (g)	1
Saturated fat (g)	neg
Unsaturated fat (g)	1
Cholesterol (mg)	0
Sodium (mg)	123
Calories	53

Makes
4 servings

TUNA & CHUTNEY DIP

This is an interestingly spicy dip or spread that makes the most of a can of tuna. Canned tuna is one of the sublime storecupboard ingredients, as are good jarred chutneys; always buy the best quality you can find of both.

INGREDIENTS

one 375g (12oz) can red tuna in brine, well drained

1 heaped tbsp hot mango chutney

1 heaped tbsp tomato chutney

1 tbsp very low-fat fromage frais

Put all the ingredients in a food processor and process to a smooth purée. Let the mixture stand for at least an hour for the flavours to develop. To serve, spread on crusty bread, or use as a dip with vegetable crudités. It is particularly good with steamed, cooled new potatoes.

Per recipe quantity

Total fat (g)	2
Saturated fat (g)	1
Unsaturated fat (g)	1
Cholesterol (mg)	179
Sodium (mg)	1381
Calories	403

Makes
300ml (½ pint)

HERBED RAITA

INGREDIENTS

handful of chopped fresh dill, thyme and tarragon

475g (15oz) very low-fat yogurt or fromage frais

zest of ½ lemon, grated

Stir the three herbs into the yogurt or fromage frais, then add the lemon zest and stir until thoroughly combined.

VARIATIONS

Use whichever herbs sound good to you: chives and parsley; mint and coriander; basil and flat-leaf parsley; or mint with peeled, deseeded, grated cucumber. To make things even more interesting, add crushed garlic marinated in a little wine vinegar. For a thicker raita, first drain the yogurt or fromage frais through a muslin-lined sieve (see page 125).

Per recipe quantity

Total fat (g)	<1
Saturated fat (g)	<1
Unsaturated fat (g)	neg
Cholesterol (mg)	10
Sodium (mg)	401
Calories	192

Makes
600ml (1 pint)

SWEETCORN CREAM DIP

Santa Fe pesto is how I think of this lively, creamy dip. Sweetcorn, roasted garlic, chillies and herbs imbue the Quark/ricotta mixture with ineffable New World flavour.

INGREDIENTS

375g (12oz) can sweetcorn kernels, drained

½–1 chilli, deseeded and finely chopped

250g (8oz) Quark

275g (9oz) ricotta

4 tbsp grated Parmesan

pulp from 1 head of roasted (or braised) garlic (see page 35)

salt and freshly ground black pepper

3 tbsp chopped fresh parsley

3 tbsp snipped fresh chives

1 Put the sweetcorn and chilli in a food processor and process to a very rough purée.

2 Add the Quark, ricotta, Parmesan, garlic and seasoning. Process again until blended but not quite smooth.

3 Stir in the herbs and process in very short bursts a few times to combine. Cover with clingfilm and chill until needed. Serve as a dip, a spread, or a garnish for thick soups – just drop a small mound on the surface of the soup.

Per recipe quantity

Total fat (g)	55
Saturated fat (g)	32
Unsaturated fat (g)	20
Cholesterol (mg)	200
Sodium (mg)	1997
Calories	1304

Makes
600ml (1 pint)

POTATO SKIN DIPPERS

*C*risp potato skin wedges are superb with dips or all by themselves, or with just a shower of black pepper and a good squeeze of fresh lemon juice.

INGREDIENTS

2 large baking potatoes

oil-water spray (see page 29)

1 Scrub the potatoes, pat dry and cut them in half lengthways.

2 Scoop out the insides, leaving a shell about 5mm (¼in) thick. (Save the scooped-out potato for another use, such as mashed potatoes or potato soup.) Cut each shell half lengthways in half.

3 Oil-spray a non-stick baking sheet, put the potato quarters, skin side down, on the sheet and spray lightly with oil-water spray. Bake in an oven preheated to 200°C/400°F/gas 6 for 25–35 minutes, until golden brown and very crisp. Serve at once.

Per serving

Total fat (g)	<1
Saturated fat (g)	neg
Unsaturated fat (g)	neg
Cholesterol (mg)	0
Sodium (mg)	10
Calories	115

Makes:
2 servings

PITTA CRISPS

*D*ips need dippers, and these pitta triangles make particularly fine ones. They are quick and easy to make, and are virtually fat-free – so much better than high-fat fried dippers.

INGREDIENTS

1 pitta bread (brown or white)

1 Cut the pitta bread into quarters or eighths. Separate each piece into two.

2 Put the pieces, in a single layer, on a non-stick baking sheet. Bake in an oven preheated to low (150°C/300°F/gas 2) for 10–15 minutes, or until the pieces of pitta bread are dried out and crisp – fat-free crisps, in fact.

Per serving

Total fat (g)	<1
Saturated fat (g)	neg
Unsaturated fat (g)	<1
Cholesterol (mg)	0
Sodium (mg)	156
Calories	80

Makes:
4 servings

SALADS & DRESSINGS

A LOW-FAT LIFESTYLE means no vinaigrette and no mayonnaise, the two high-fat staples of salad making. But there is no need to make do with just an acetic squeeze of lemon juice. My non-fat vinaigrettes (a contradiction in terms, I know, but I'm bending the rules here) dress salads with great style. Mixtures of exquisite vinegars and citrus juices can make lovely dressings, and my Not Mayo, which is based on fromage frais, stands in very successfully for the wickedly high-fat, egg-based real thing.

ASPARAGUS WITH CREAMY PRAWN DRESSING
mixes luxury ingredients for a superb salad.

DRESSING BASE

The rich, creamy dressing for this salad has an infusion of high-flavoured ingredients as its base. Rapid simmering reduces the infusion to a thick pulp which is mixed with lightly spiced fromage frais and prawns.

LEMON JUICE

LEMON RIND

GARLIC

SPRING ONION

VEGETABLE STOCK

WHITE VERMOUTH

TERIYAKI SAUCE

WORCESTERSHIRE SAUCE

ASPARAGUS WITH A CREAMY PRAWN DRESSING

INGREDIENTS

5cm (2in) strip of lemon rind

350ml (12fl oz) stock (see page 30)

125ml (4fl oz) dry white vermouth

10 garlic cloves, lightly crushed

6 spring onions, trimmed and chopped

lemon juice, to taste

dash or two each of Teriyaki and Worcestershire sauces

500g (1lb) tiger prawns, peeled

2 tbsp fromage frais

1 tsp red pepper Dijon mustard

dash of Tabasco sauce

salt and freshly ground black pepper

2–3 tbsp each chopped fresh basil and parsley

2 bunches asparagus, trimmed, peeled and steamed (see page 78)

½ cucumber, peeled, deseeded and sliced into thin crescents

300g (10oz) cherry tomatoes, halved

1 Put the lemon rind, 300ml (½ pint) of stock, the vermouth, garlic, spring onions, a few drops of lemon juice, and the Teriyaki and Worcestershire sauces in a pan. Bring to the boil, stirring occasionally, and cook until the garlic is tender and falling apart, and the liquid is reduced to a glaze.

2 Discard the lemon rind. Take the pan off the heat and mash the mixture inside with a potato masher. Transfer to a bowl.

3 In the same pan (no need to wash it) bring the remaining stock to the boil with a few drops of lemon juice. Add the prawns and cook, stirring, for 2–3 minutes, until just done. Drain, refresh under cold water and drain again.

4 Whisk the fromage frais with the mustard. Add a dash each of Tabasco and Worcestershire sauces, the garlic mixture, prawns, and seasoning. Fold in the herbs.

5 Arrange the asparagus on a platter. Pile the creamy prawns over the stem ends and arrange the cucumber and tomatoes all around.

Per main course serving	
Total fat (g)	2
Saturated fat (g)	<1
Unsaturated fat (g)	1
Cholesterol (mg)	244
Sodium (mg)	405
Calories	153

Makes
6 servings as a first course, 4 as a main course

ROASTED BEETROOT, ORANGE & ROCKET SALAD

The earthy sweetness of the beetroot and the bitterness of the rocket in this salad, not to mention their dark red and deep green colours, make a stunning combination.

INGREDIENTS

125g (4oz) rocket leaves

four 125g (4oz) oven-roasted beetroots (see page 78), peeled and sliced

2 blood oranges (or 2 ordinary seedless oranges), peeled and cut into thin slices

5 tbsp Beetroot Vinaigrette (see page 59)

salt and freshly ground black pepper

chopped flat-leaf parsley, to garnish

1 Line a platter with rocket leaves. Slice the beetroot and overlap, interspersing with orange slices here and there, on the leaves.

2 Drizzle on the vinaigrette and season with salt and pepper. Garnish the salad with parsley before serving.

Per serving

Total fat (g)	0.5
Saturated fat (g)	0
Unsaturated fat (g)	0.5
Cholesterol (mg)	0
Sodium (mg)	129
Calories	85

Makes
4 servings

CANNELLINI BEAN & CHICKPEA SALAD

Another vibrantly coloured salad, this is also quick to make since it combines two pulses that are available in cans – no need to soak overnight.

INGREDIENTS

2 garlic cloves, crushed

½–1 chilli pepper, deseeded and finely diced

½ red onion, chopped

juice of 1 large orange

juice of 1 lime

2 tbsp lemon juice

pinch of sugar

1 tbsp balsamic vinegar

3 small carrots

1 large yellow pepper

2–3 inner stalks celery, leaves and all

4 small, ripe vine tomatoes

475g (15oz) can chickpeas, drained and rinsed

475g (15oz) can cannellini beans, drained and rinsed

salt and freshly ground black pepper

60g (2oz) baby spinach leaves

60g (2oz) watercress leaves

chopped flat-leaf parsley and shredded mint, to garnish

1 Put the garlic, chilli pepper, onion, citrus juices, sugar and balsamic vinegar into a large bowl and stir together well. Leave the dressing to marinate while you prepare the vegetables.

2 Peel and dice the carrots, and skin, deseed and dice the pepper (see page 34). Peel and chop the celery, and deseed and dice the tomatoes.

3 Toss the vegetables in the dressing in the bowl. Add the chickpeas and cannellini beans and stir with two spoons to mix well. Season with salt and pepper. Leave in the refrigerator for a few hours or overnight to allow the flavours to blend.

4 To serve, line a platter with baby spinach and watercress leaves. Heap the vegetables and beans on the leaves, and garnish with the herbs.

Per serving

Total fat (g)	3
Saturated fat (g)	0.5
Unsaturated fat (g)	2
Cholesterol (mg)	0
Sodium (mg)	542
Calories	198

Makes
6 servings

COUSCOUS VEGETABLE SALAD

Couscous, mixed with one of the wonderful no-fat vinaigrettes and lavishly strewn with crisp vegetables, then surrounded by red onions and chillies, makes a visually dazzling side-salad or vegetarian main course.

INGREDIENTS

For the couscous

180g (6oz) couscous

250ml (8fl oz) well seasoned stock (see page 30)

For the relish

1 small red onion, finely chopped

1 chilli, deseeded and finely chopped

1 tbsp balsamic vinegar

juice of 1 lime and ½ orange

8–10 ripe vine tomatoes, cut into quarters or eighths

For the vegetables

½ cucumber, peeled, halved, deseeded, and sliced

2 inner celery stalks with leaves, sliced

1 red pepper, skinned, deseeded and diced (see page 34)

1 yellow pepper, skinned, deseeded and diced (see page 34)

2 small courgettes, trimmed and diced

For the dressing and garnish

1 quantity Sun-dried Tomato Vinaigrette (see Basic Vinaigrette variations, page 59)

1 tbsp each chopped fresh flat-leaf parsley and mint, to garnish

1 To make the couscous, bring the stock to the boil. Put the couscous in a bowl, then pour over the stock and mix well. Cover and leave for 10–15 minutes, until the couscous is tender and the liquid has been absorbed. Fluff with a fork.

2 Mix together all the relish ingredients except the tomatoes. Leave to marinate for 10 minutes.

3 For the vegetables, put all the prepared ingredients in a bowl, drizzle in 2–3 tablespoons of the vinaigrette, and stir together gently with two spoons.

4 To assemble the salad, mix the couscous with half the vegetables and about 150ml (¼ pint) of the vinaigrette. Pile on to a platter and surround with the remaining vegetables.

5 Gently mix together the relish mixture and the tomatoes and arrange around the outer perimeter of the platter. Finally, sprinkle the freshly chopped parsley and mint over the dish.

 Per serving

Total fat (g)	2
Saturated fat (g)	neg
Unsaturated fat (g)	1
Cholesterol (mg)	0
Sodium (mg)	248
Calories	202

 Makes
4 servings

TOMATO, PEACH & GRILLED PEPPER SALAD

I give specific quantities for the ingredients in this wonderfully Technicolored salad, but amounts can be varied to suit your own taste or what is in season.

INGREDIENTS

2 ripe tomatoes, sliced

2 ripe peaches, halved, stoned and sliced

1 each red and orange peppers, grilled and skinned (see page 35)

salt and freshly ground black pepper

1 tbsp chopped fresh flat-leaf parsley

1 tbsp shredded fresh basil

½ quantity Grilled Pepper Vinaigrette (see page 59)

1 Alternate slices of tomato, peach and roasted pepper on an attractive platter.

2 Season the salad lightly with salt and pepper, then strew on the parsley and basil. Serve the vinaigrette separately.

 Per serving

Total fat (g)	1
Saturated fat (g)	neg
Unsaturated fat (g)	1
Cholesterol (mg)	0
Sodium (mg)	203
Calories	68

 Makes
4 servings

NOT MAYO

Real mayonnaise is an emulsion of egg yolk and oil – just thinking about it strikes terror in my heart. Instead, try this fromage frais dressing. Not mayo – no, indeed – but wonderfully creamy and delicious all the same, especially as a sandwich spread.

INGREDIENTS

1 tbsp Dijon mustard

500g (1lb) very low fat fromage frais

Gently whisk the mustard into the fromage frais.

VARIATIONS

Flavoured mustards work well, too – try Red Pepper and Garlic Provençal Mustard instead of the basic Dijon mustard. The following may also be added (in small quantities at a time, until you reach the flavour you prefer): puréed roasted garlic (see page 35) or pan-braised garlic (see page 78); a drizzle of balsamic vinegar; chopped fresh herbs; puréed grilled pepper (see page 35); puréed mango or peach (with a little balsamic vinegar).

Per recipe quantity

Total fat (g)	2
Saturated fat (g)	1
Unsaturated fat (g)	1
Cholesterol (mg)	6
Sodium (mg)	641
Calories	369

Makes
600ml (1 pint)

VINAIGRETTE BASE

This mixture, based on balsamic vinegar and citrus juices with slivered black olives to give the unique flavour of olive oil, forms the base for countless no-oil vinaigrettes. It will keep for a week in the refrigerator.

INGREDIENTS

125ml (4fl oz) balsamic vinegar

125ml (4fl oz) lime juice

125ml (4fl oz) orange juice

2 garlic cloves, crushed

3 black olives, slivered off their stones

1 tbsp Dijon mustard, or Red Pepper and Garlic Provençal mustard

pinch of sugar

Mix all the ingredients together in a screw-top jar, put on the lid and shake well. Store in the refrigerator until needed.

VARIATIONS

Sun-dried Tomato Vinaigrette: mix 2 tablespoons of the vinaigrette base with 90ml (3fl oz) water and 2 sun-dried tomatoes and simmer until the tomatoes are plump, and the liquid is almost evaporated. Put into a blender with the remaining vinaigrette base, and process until smooth.

Mango Vinaigrette: put a quarter of the flesh of a large mango in a blender with the vinaigrette base and process until well mixed.

Grilled Pepper Vinaigrette: put ½ grilled pepper (see page 35) or ½ canned or jarred pepper, drained, in a blender. Add 1 quantity of the vinaigrette base and blend the mixture until smooth.

Beetroot Vinaigrette: chop half of a whole roasted beetroot (see page 78). Put in a blender with 1 quantity of the vinaigrette base and process until smooth.

Pear Vinaigrette: peel and dice half a juicy, ripe pear. Put in a blender with 1 quantity of the vinaigrette base and process until the mixture is smooth.

Per recipe quantity

Total fat (g)	2
Saturated fat (g)	neg
Unsaturated fat (g)	2
Cholesterol (mg)	0
Sodium (mg)	684
Calories	95

Makes
300ml (½ pint)

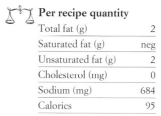

SAUCES & SALSAS

A GOOD COLLECTION OF SAUCES used to include all of the classic emulsion sauces, such as hollandaise, béarnaise and beurre blanc sauces, roux-based white sauces, olive oil-heavy tomato sauces, in fact a catalogue of high-fat techniques. But times change. Vegetable sauces and flavour infusions deliver texture and taste, salsas – jewelled clusters of fresh and vibrant vegetables and fruits – provide verve. And how exciting it is to indulge in that most modern of pastimes, the mixing of culinary metaphors. Why *not* a Chinese/Mexican salsa, or a Thai/Italian tomato sauce? Decide for yourself with the recipes here.

TORTILLAS LAYERED WITH SALSAS *combine colour and flavour in extravagant style.*

Using Salsas

The tortilla stack opposite is an imaginative mix of several recipes. From the top, the fillings are Mango & Fennel Salsa (see below), a layer of chargrilled peppers, Cherry Tomato & Red Onion Salsa (see below), Green Pea Guacamole (see page 50), Silky Stir-fried Pepper Strips (see page 71) and Grilled Aubergines & Courgettes (see page 81).

CHERRY TOMATO & RED ONION SALSA

GREEN PEA GUACAMOLE

MANGO & FENNEL SALSA

Cherry Tomato & Red Onion Salsa

This very simple salsa includes wedges of ripe tomatoes rather than tomato pulp, giving it an interesting texture. It makes a colourful garnish: try it with Grilled Aubergine & Courgette Slices (see page 81), for instance.

INGREDIENTS

1 garlic clove, crushed

1 tbsp lime juice

juice of ½ orange

1 tbsp lemon juice

½ red onion, diced

1 tbsp balsamic vinegar

8 vine tomatoes

2 spring onions, sliced

1 tbsp each chopped fresh parsley, mint and coriander

salt

1 Put the garlic, citrus juices, red onion and balsamic vinegar in a large bowl, mix well and leave to stand for 15–30 minutes.

2 Cut the tomatoes into quarters or eighths (depending on size) and add to the bowl. Scatter in the spring onions and herbs. Season with a little salt and toss gently with two spoons until combined.

 Per serving

Total fat (g)	<1
Saturated fat (g)	neg
Unsaturated fat (g)	neg
Cholesterol (mg)	0
Sodium (mg)	42
Calories	23

Makes
6 servings

Mango & Fennel Salsa

The distinctively different yet complementary flavours of mango and fennel make this salsa memorable. It makes an excellent accompaniment for meats, particularly pork and poultry.

INGREDIENTS

1 tbsp balsamic vinegar

1 tbsp lime juice

1 garlic clove, crushed

1 red chilli, deseeded and finely chopped

1 mango, diced (see page 136)

1 head fennel, trimmed and diced, feathery fronds reserved and snipped

½ cucumber, peeled, deseeded and diced

1 small red onion, diced

3 spring onions, sliced

2–3 tbsp each chopped fresh coriander and flat-leaf parsley

2–3 tbsp shredded fresh mint

1 Put the vinegar, lime juice, garlic and chilli in a bowl, mix well and leave to marinate for 10–15 minutes.

2 Add the mango, the fennel (with a scattering of snipped fennel fronds), the cucumber, onions and herbs. Mix with two spoons, gently tossing together all the ingredients.

 Per serving

Total fat (g)	<1
Saturated fat (g)	neg
Unsaturated fat (g)	neg
Cholesterol (mg)	0
Sodium (mg)	7
Calories	53

Makes
6 servings

BOLOGNESE SAUCE

Although this is not a "real" Bolognese Sauce (as soon as you eliminate the added fat, you break all the rules of traditional cooking), it is a deeply satisfying, meaty sauce with lots of flavour, thanks to the aubergine infusion. It's wonderful with tagliatelle or linguine but it works well with pastas like lasagne or cannelloni, too.

INGREDIENTS

2 aubergines, each about 375g (12oz), trimmed, peeled and diced (see pages 36–37)

2 red onions, chopped

2 garlic cloves, crushed

3 sun-dried tomatoes, chopped

pinch or 2 of dried chilli flakes (optional)

3 black olives, slivered off their stones

approximately 300ml (½ pint) stock (see page 30), plus extra as needed

4 tbsp dry red wine

500g (1lb) extra-lean minced meat (pork or beef)

two 425g (14oz) cans chopped tomatoes

salt and freshly ground black pepper

1 In a heavy-based frying pan, combine all the ingredients up to the meat. Cover and simmer briskly for 5–7 minutes. Uncover and cook, stirring occasionally, until the aubergine is very tender and the liquid is absorbed, adding a little more stock if needed. Remove from the heat, leave to cool slightly then purée in a food processor or blender.

2 Meanwhile, sauté the meat in a non-stick frying pan, breaking it up with a wooden spoon. Drain off any fat. Combine the meat and aubergine mixture in the frying pan, add the tomatoes, with their juice, and season to taste. Simmer briskly, uncovered, for about 10 minutes, until thickened.

Per recipe quantity

Total fat (g)	25
Saturated fat (g)	8
Unsaturated fat (g)	15
Cholesterol (mg)	300
Sodium (mg)	1157
Calories	1049

Makes
1.5 litres (2½ pints)

TOMATO AUBERGINE SAUCE

This combination of tomatoes and aubergines, enhanced by an almost Indian mix of spices and lemon juice, makes a rich, velvety, complex sauce that is excellent with pasta or as a bed for fish fillets.

INGREDIENTS

2 aubergines, peeled and chopped (see pages 36–37)

2 red onions, chopped

8 garlic cloves, crushed and peeled

4 black olives, slivered off their stones

¼–½ tsp dried chilli flakes, to taste

1 tbsp ground cumin

1 tbsp ground coriander

2 tsp ground paprika

1 tsp ground turmeric

pinch sugar, plus extra to taste

2 tbsp lemon juice, plus extra to taste

175ml (6fl oz) dry red wine

300ml (½ pint) stock (see page 30)

four 425g (14oz) cans chopped tomatoes

salt and freshly ground black pepper

2–3 tbsp fresh herbs such as coriander, flat-leaf parsley or mint, chopped or shredded

1 Combine all the ingredients except the tomatoes, seasoning and herbs in a wok or frying pan. Cover, and simmer briskly for 7–10 minutes, then uncover and simmer until the aubergines and onions are meltingly tender, and the liquid is absorbed.

2 Add the tomatoes and salt and pepper. Simmer, partially covered, for 15–20 minutes, until thickened. Leave to cool slightly.

3 Using a blender, purée the sauce in small batches until velvety smooth. The sauce may be prepared up to this point then refrigerated or frozen.

4 When ready to use, bring the sauce to a simmer. Taste, and add seasoning or more lemon juice or a further pinch of sugar, as needed. Stir in the herbs and simmer for 5 minutes more.

Per recipe quantity

Total fat (g)	11
Saturated fat (g)	2
Unsaturated fat (g)	8
Cholesterol (mg)	0
Sodium (mg)	1250
Calories	590

Makes
2 litres (3½ pints)

BOLOGNESE SAUCE

SICILIAN VEGETABLE SALSA

TOMATO AUBERGINE SAUCE

BASIL PESTO

SICILIAN VEGETABLE SALSA

This splendidly herby vegetable stew is based on the Arabian-influenced sweet and sour vegetable conserves of Sicily (with a few olives standing in for olive oil). It is a good accompaniment for Lemon-garlic Roasted Chicken (see page 84) or Crusty Grill-fried Pork Escalopes (see page 95).

INGREDIENTS

1 courgette, coarsely chopped

1 red onion, coarsely chopped

2 garlic cloves, crushed and peeled

1 chilli, chopped

4 sun-dried tomatoes, chopped

4 black olives, slivered off their stones

1 tbsp capers, drained

2 tbsp sultanas

1 head fennel, trimmed and coarsely chopped

1 red pepper, peeled and deseeded (see pages 34–35)

1 tbsp balsamic vinegar

4 tbsp lemon juice, plus extra to taste

juice of ½ orange

slivered rind of ¼ lemon

salt and freshly ground black pepper

4 tomatoes, skinned, deseeded and cut into strips

1 tbsp chopped fresh flat-leaf parsley

½ tbsp chopped fresh oregano

1 tbsp torn basil leaves

1 Combine all the ingredients except the tomatoes and herbs in a wok. Simmer, stirring occasionally, until the vegetables are just tender and the liquid is greatly reduced.

2 Stir in the tomatoes and simmer for 5–10 minutes until the mixture is thick and the tomatoes have broken down. Taste, and add more seasoning and lemon juice to taste.

3 Leave to cool slightly, then stir in the herbs. Serve as a main course with an accompanying mound of Garlic and Lemon Roasted Potatoes (see page 74), or as a first course with crusty bread.

Per serving

Total fat (g)	<1
Saturated fat (g)	neg
Unsaturated fat (g)	<1
Cholesterol (mg)	0
Sodium (mg)	76
Calories	55

Makes
900ml (1½ pints)
(6 servings)

WHITE PESTO

White Pesto is a creamy garlic spread – dynamite on crusty bread, but also good folded into freshly cooked pasta shapes such as penne or pennoni.

INGREDIENTS

200g (7oz) Quark

30g (1oz) pine nuts

75g (2½oz) freshly grated Parmesan

about 12 cloves of Pan-braised Garlic (see page 78)

Purée all the ingredients together in a food processor or blender until smooth. Cover with clingfilm and store in the refrigerator.

VARIATION

For Creamy Basil Pesto, add a few handfuls of fresh basil and flat-leaf parsley before processing.

Per recipe quantity

Total fat (g)	45
Saturated fat (g)	17
Unsaturated fat (g)	26
Cholesterol (mg)	77
Sodium (mg)	908
Calories	705

Makes
300ml (½ pint)

PEPPER SAUCE

There are many possibilities for jewel-coloured sauces, using red or yellow peppers. I like to use sauces of both colours as a bed for fish, poultry, grill-fried aubergines and courgettes, and grilled meat dishes.

INGREDIENTS

10 yellow or red peppers, unpeeled and coarsely chopped

2 garlic cloves, crushed

6 spring onions, trimmed and sliced

1 chilli, deseeded and diced (optional)

½ tbsp paprika (with red peppers only)

300ml (½ pint) stock (see page 30)

salt and freshly ground black pepper

1 Put all the ingredients except the salt and pepper in a heavy-based frying pan. Bring to the boil, then reduce the heat and simmer for 20–30 minutes, until the vegetables are tender.

2 Season with salt and pepper. Leave to cool slightly.

3 Purée the mixture in batches in a food processor or blender. Strain through a sieve or strainer, rubbing it through with a wooden spoon. Discard the tough skins left behind in the sieve.

4 Return the sauce to the pan and simmer until the sauce is thick enough to coat the back of a spoon. Taste and adjust the seasoning, if necessary.

Per recipe quantity

Total fat (g)	4
Saturated fat (g)	1
Unsaturated fat (g)	2
Cholesterol (mg)	0
Sodium (mg)	319
Calories	371

Makes
900ml (1½ pints)

TOMATO, GARLIC & PEPPER SAUCE

This is an interesting variant of homemade tomato sauce, rich with simmered garlic and puréed pepper, piquant and fragrant with chillies and lime juice. It makes a glorious pasta sauce, but it is even better as a bed for grilled meat, poultry or fish.

INGREDIENTS

2 red onions, roughly chopped

8 garlic cloves, lightly crushed

4 sun-dried tomatoes, chopped

4 black olives, slivered off their stones

500g (1lb) red peppers, peeled, deseeded and roughly chopped (see page 34)

1 tsp ground cumin

½ tsp ground coriander

pinch or two of dried chilli flakes

300ml (½ pint) vegetable stock (see page 30), plus extra as needed

300ml (½ pint) dry red wine

four 425g (14oz) cans chopped tomatoes, or 1.75kg (3½lb) fresh tomatoes, skinned, deseeded and diced

salt and freshly ground black pepper

pinch of sugar (optional)

juice of 1 lime

chopped fresh herbs, to garnish

1 Put all the ingredients, up to and including the red wine, in a wok or heavy-based saucepan. Cover, bring to the boil and simmer briskly for 10 minutes.

2 Uncover and continue to simmer for a few minutes until the garlic, onions and peppers are tender and the liquid is greatly reduced. Make sure the mixture remains moist: add a little more liquid if needed. When tender, the vegetables should be "frying" in their own juices.

3 Stir in the tomatoes, salt and pepper, and a pinch of sugar if the tomatoes are particularly acidic. Simmer for 10–15 minutes, until thickened. Add the lime juice, and more seasoning as needed.

4 Pour the mixture into a blender, and blend to a purée. Check the seasoning once more.

5 Add plenty of chopped fresh herbs, either leaving them as a garnish on the sauce, or stirring them into it.

Per recipe quantity

Total fat (g)	8
Saturated fat (g)	1
Unsaturated fat (g)	5
Cholesterol (mg)	0
Sodium (mg)	1256
Calories	651

Makes
2 litres (3½ pints)

GRILLED PEPPER & OREGANO PISTOU

This is a vivid, rough pepper purée to be used by the dollop, as a garnish for soups and stews. It adds great visual pizzazz, as well as a jolt of flavour.

INGREDIENTS

2 large peppers, grilled, skinned and diced (see page 35)

2–3 cloves Pan-braised Garlic (see page 78)

2 tbsp fresh oregano leaves

1 tbsp chopped fresh flat-leaf parsley

½–1 tsp Sambal Oelek (Indonesian hot chilli paste), to taste

2–3 tbsp freshly grated Parmesan

1 Combine all the ingredients in a food processor, and process to a rough purée.

2 Cover with clingfilm and refrigerate. This sauce can be stored for several days.

Per recipe quantity

Total fat (g)	14
Saturated fat (g)	8
Unsaturated fat (g)	6
Cholesterol (mg)	37
Sodium (mg)	485
Calories	312

Makes
garnish for 3–4 dishes

ROASTED VEGETABLE SALSA

This salsa makes a fabulous dip with Pitta Crisps (see page 53), fat-free potato crisps, oven-fried potato wedges, oven-fried potato skins or fat-free tortilla chips. It also makes a colourful and tempting garnish for many dishes in this book, including Crusty "Grill-fried" Pork Escalopes (see page 95) and Spicy Citrus-scented Mexican Sausages (see page 94)

INGREDIENTS

2 aubergines, each about 250g (8oz)

1 large head garlic, plus 2 garlic cloves, crushed

2 red peppers, grilled, skinned and diced (see page 35)

1 chilli, deseeded and chopped

1 small red onion, chopped

2 sun-dried tomatoes, finely chopped

1 tbsp each lemon, orange and lime juice

1 tbsp balsamic vinegar

4 ripe tomatoes, skinned, deseeded and diced

4 spring onions, halved lengthways and thinly sliced

6 tbsp chopped fresh flat-leaf parsley

4 tbsp torn fresh mint leaves

salt and freshly ground black pepper

1 Prick the aubergines in several places with a fork or thin skewer. Remove the papery outer covering of the whole head of garlic, but do not separate the cloves. Wrap the garlic in foil.

2 Bake the aubergines and garlic directly on the oven shelf of a preheated oven for 45–55 minutes, until the aubergine is soft and collapsed, and the garlic is tender inside. Remove from the oven and put on a wire rack to cool.

3 Meanwhile, put the diced peppers, 2 crushed garlic cloves, chilli, red onion, sun-dried tomatoes, citrus juices and vinegar in a bowl and leave to marinate.

4 When the aubergines and garlic are cool enough to handle, remove and discard the stem and skin from the aubergines. Roughly chop the flesh, and scrape into a food processor bowl.

5 Separate the roasted garlic cloves and squeeze each one over the bowl so that the puréed garlic pops out.

6 Add the remaining ingredients, and the vegetables with their marinade. Season with salt and pepper and process to a rough purée.

Per serving

Total fat (g)	1
Saturated fat (g)	neg
Unsaturated fat (g)	1
Cholesterol (mg)	0
Sodium (mg)	15
Calories	68

Oven temperature
190°C/375°F/gas 5

Cooking time
45–55 minutes

Makes
600ml (1 pint) or 4 servings

TOMATO SAUCE

The secret of a good very low-fat tomato sauce is in the flavour infusion: it guarantees richness and depth. It is worth making the sauce in large quantities, and then freezing it in batches. With a sauce like this to hand, all sorts of glorious meals are possible.

INGREDIENTS

2 red onions, chopped

4 sun-dried tomatoes, chopped

4 black olives, slivered off their stones

pinch or two of dried chilli flakes, to taste

4 garlic cloves, crushed

175ml (6fl oz) stock (see page 30)

175ml (6fl oz) red wine

four 425g (14oz) cans chopped tomatoes

pinch of sugar (optional)

salt and freshly ground black pepper

1–2 tbsp tomato purée

3 tbsp fresh herbs such as chopped flat-leaf parsley, oregano or shredded basil

1 Put the onions, sun-dried tomatoes, olives, chilli flakes, garlic, stock and wine in a wok or frying pan. Cover and simmer briskly for 5–7 minutes, then uncover and simmer until the onions are tender, and the liquid is almost evaporated.

2 Stir in the chopped tomatoes and their juice, and sugar if the tomatoes are very acidic. Season with salt and pepper and simmer, partially covered, for 15–20 minutes.

3 Stir in the tomato purée and simmer for 5–10 minutes more. The sauce may be prepared up to this point, then chilled for several days or frozen.

4 When ready to serve, bring the sauce to a simmer and stir in the herbs. Check the seasoning and add more salt and pepper, if needed. Simmer for 5 minutes, then serve.

VARIATION

Arrabbiata Sauce: increase the garlic cloves to 8–10 according to your taste, and substitute 1–2 chopped chillies for the dried chilli flakes.

 Per recipe quantity

Total fat (g)	5
Saturated fat (g)	1
Unsaturated fat (g)	3
Cholesterol (mg)	0
Sodium (mg)	1176
Calories	464

Makes
1 litre (1¼ pints)

BLACK BEAN TOMATO SAUCE

Use storecupboard ingredients to whip together this Oriental-inspired sauce. Serve the sauce to great effect with fish steaks or fillets, pork tenderloin or grilled duck breasts.

INGREDIENTS

4 garlic cloves, peeled

2.5cm (1in) piece fresh root ginger

6–7 spring onions, trimmed and chopped

300ml (½ pint) stock (see page 30)

60ml (2fl oz) dry sherry

1 tbsp oyster sauce

1 tsp Chinese chilli sauce

2 tbsp Chinese black bean sauce

125ml (4fl oz) passata

juice of 1 lime

2 tbsp chopped fresh coriander

1 Crush together the garlic cloves and the ginger and put into a wok with the chopped spring onions, stock and sherry. Simmer briskly until the liquid is almost evaporated.

2 Stir in the oyster, chilli and black bean sauces and bring to the boil. Continue to boil, stirring, for a few seconds.

3 Stir in the passata, and then simmer briskly for 30 seconds. Stir in the lime juice and chopped coriander and simmer for a few seconds further.

 Per recipe quantity

Total fat (g)	2
Saturated fat (g)	1
Unsaturated fat (g)	1
Cholesterol (mg)	0
Sodium (mg)	2082
Calories	199

Makes
300ml (½ pint)

CHINESE TOMATO SALSA

Wed a chunky Mexican salsa to Chinese seasonings for an explosion of flavour. This non-traditional salsa is a terrific accompaniment for fish, pasta and meatballs.

INGREDIENTS

2 garlic cloves, crushed

2.5cm (1in) piece fresh root ginger, peeled and crushed

3 tbsp rice vinegar

375g (12oz) cherry tomatoes

6 spring onions, trimmed and chopped

2–3 tbsp chopped fresh coriander

1 tsp sugar

1 tsp Chinese chilli sauce

1 Put the garlic, ginger and rice vinegar in a bowl large enough to hold the whole salsa and leave to marinate for about 30 minutes.

2 Cut the cherry tomatoes into halves or quarters, according to taste, and add them with the spring onions, coriander, sugar and Chinese chilli sauce to the marinated ingredients. Mix everything together thoroughly before using.

 Per serving

Total fat (g)	<1
Saturated fat (g)	neg
Unsaturated fat (g)	<1
Cholesterol (mg)	0
Sodium (mg)	50
Calories	30

Makes
300ml (½ pint) or
4 servings

WHITE BEAN, ORANGE & TARRAGON PUREE

I like this dolloped on to servings of soups or vegetable purées, but it works as a dip or spread as well. Change the herbs to your taste; if you don't like tarragon, try flat-leaf parsley or mint instead.

INGREDIENTS

425g (14oz) canned cannellini beans, drained and rinsed

1½ tbsp snipped fresh tarragon

1 tbsp Red Pepper Garlic Mustard

½ tbsp tomato purée

4–5 cloves Pan-braised Garlic (see page 78)

juice of ½ large orange

2 tbsp lemon juice, plus extra to taste

dash or two of Tabasco sauce

salt and freshly ground black pepper

Purée all of the ingredients together in a food processor or blender. Taste, and add more citrus juices, Tabasco sauce, and salt and pepper, according to personal preference.

 Per recipe quantity

Total fat (g)	4
Saturated fat (g)	1
Unsaturated fat (g)	3
Cholesterol (mg)	0
Sodium (mg)	2150
Calories	370

Makes
300ml (½ pint)

WHITE BEAN, ORANGE & TARRAGON PUREE

TOMATO SAUCE

BLACK BEAN TOMATO SAUCE

VEGETABLES

VEGETABLES LIE AT THE HEART of a healthy low-fat lifestyle. They make food beautiful to look at and delicious to eat. And, of course, they are life-enhancingly nutritious. Enrich your menus with an exciting mix of main course vegetable dishes and vegetable accompaniments. Why not plan all-vegetable meals once in a while, mixing and matching several recipes from this collection? A beautifully coordinated feast of vegetables is the fresh, modern way to create a meal.

CAULIFLOWER STIR-FRIED IN RED WINE
takes on a pretty sunset-pink colour and a rich flavour as it cooks.

A FLAVOUR INFUSION FOR STIR-FRYING

The flavour infusion for this recipe, made up of fresh chilli, garlic, olives, sun-dried tomatoes and onion, with wine and stock providing the liquid, needs only a short initial simmering before the main ingredients are added.

VEGETABLE STOCK

DRY RED WINE

RED CHILLI

GARLIC

BLACK OLIVES

SUN-DRIED TOMATOES

RED ONION

CAULIFLOWER STIR-FRIED IN RED WINE

INGREDIENTS

4 black olives, slivered off their stones

4 sun-dried tomatoes, chopped

1 large red onion, cut into wedges

pinch of dried chilli flakes, or more to taste

4 large garlic cloves, crushed

150ml (¼ pint) dry red wine

300ml (½ pint) stock (see page 30)

4 red peppers, grilled, skinned (see page 35) and cut into 1cm (½in) strips

2 cauliflowers, broken into florets

salt and freshly ground black pepper

4 tbsp lemon juice

chopped fresh flat-leaf parsley or oregano, to garnish

1 Put the olive pieces, sun-dried tomatoes, onion wedges, chilli flakes, garlic, red wine and 150ml (¼ pint) of stock in a non-stick wok. Cover the wok, bring to the boil and simmer briskly for 5 minutes.

2 Uncover the wok and add the peppers. Stir, and simmer briskly for 2–3 minutes.

3 Add the cauliflower florets and the remaining stock. Season with salt and pepper, cover and simmer briskly for 5 minutes, stirring occasionally.

4 Uncover the wok, then sprinkle over approximately 2 tablespoons of lemon juice. Continue to simmer, uncovered, until the cauliflower is tender, and the liquid has reduced by two-thirds.

5 Taste, adding the remaining lemon juice and adjusting the seasoning to taste. Sprinkle over the fresh parsley or oregano and serve.

Per serving

Total fat (g)	3
Saturated fat (g)	1
Unsaturated fat (g)	2
Cholesterol (mg)	0
Sodium (mg)	167
Calories	173

Makes
4 servings

GLAZED FENNEL

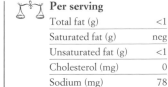

Looking a little like bulbous celery, but with a distinctive haunting anise flavour, fennel is a vegetable to be cherished. Crunchy, raw fennel in a salad is a great pleasure; fennel stir-fried in stock and lemon until meltingly tender and glazed is memorable. Illustrated on pages 113 and 151.

INGREDIENTS

3 fennel bulbs, stalks and outer layer trimmed and fronds reserved

2 tbsp lemon juice

150–175ml (5–6fl oz) stock (see page 30)

salt and freshly ground black pepper

1 large orange, peeled and chopped

2 black Calamata olives, slivered off their stones

1 Cut the fennel bulbs in half lengthways, then slice across into 1cm (½in) slices.

2 Put the fennel into a frying pan or wok with the lemon juice and 125ml (4fl oz) of stock. Season with salt and pepper and stir-fry over a high heat until the fennel is tender, but not mushy, and glazed with the reduced stock. Add a little more stock as needed.

3 Snip the fennel fronds finely and stir them in with the orange pieces and the olives. Serve hot as an accompaniment, as a topping for grilled polenta squares, or as an omelette filling.

 Per serving

Total fat (g)	<1
Saturated fat (g)	neg
Unsaturated fat (g)	<1
Cholesterol (mg)	0
Sodium (mg)	78
Calories	36

Makes
4 servings

SWEET & SOUR RED ONIONS

Red onion slices, gently braised in a sweet, sour and spicy mixture of balsamic vinegar, Dijon mustard and stock, make a great sandwich filling, a garnish for steak or fish, or a topping for sausages. Illustrated on pages 113 and 151.

INGREDIENTS

6 red onions, peeled and halved lengthways

450–500ml (15–16fl oz) stock (see page 30)

½ tsp Dijon mustard

1½ tbsp balsamic vinegar

1 tbsp sugar

2 garlic cloves, crushed

pinch of dried chilli flakes

1 Cut the onion halves lengthways into 1cm (½in) slices. Place in a lidded frying pan with the remaining ingredients over a medium-high heat.

2 Bring the mixture to the boil, then reduce the heat, cover and simmer, stirring occasionally, for about 10 minutes.

3 Remove the cover and continue to simmer, stirring frequently, until the onions are nicely glazed and tender, but still a little crunchy.

 Per serving

Total fat (g)	1
Saturated fat (g)	neg
Unsaturated fat (g)	1
Cholesterol (mg)	0
Sodium (mg)	126
Calories	143

Makes
4 servings

SILKY STIR-FRIED SWEET PEPPER STRIPS

Stir-fried in stock or in a mixture of stock and wine, pepper strips have a tender suppleness, sweetness and colour that make them pure pleasure on the plate.

INGREDIENTS

6 red peppers, halved, cored and deseeded

175ml (6fl oz) stock (see page 30)

freshly ground black pepper

1 Cut each of the pepper halves into their natural sections, then peel each piece using a swivel-bladed vegetable peeler. Cut each peeled piece into strips about 1cm (½in) wide.

2 Put the peppers and the stock in a heavy-based frying pan, and set over a medium-high heat. Add the black pepper and bring to the boil.

3 Gently toss the peppers in the hot stock and continue to cook until the liquid has reduced by two-thirds.

4 Turn down the heat slightly and sauté the peppers in their juices for a few minutes, until they are very tender and a thick sauce has formed.

5 Serve as crostini, with the pepper strips and pan juices piled on to garlic-rubbed, toasted slices of rustic bread. This dish would also work well served as a garnish, as part of a platter of mixed antipasti, or as a vegetable accompaniment to fish.

Per serving

Total fat (g)	1
Saturated fat (g)	neg
Unsaturated fat (g)	1
Cholesterol (mg)	0
Sodium (mg)	48
Calories	79

Makes
4 servings

OVEN-FRIED POTATOES

All you need for the most wonderful oven-fried potatoes – wedges, sticks, slices, whatever you prefer – are unpeeled potatoes, either big baking potatoes or small new potatoes, oil-water spray and a non-stick baking sheet. Cooked this way, potatoes are exquisite: crunchy on the outside, fluffy and tender within, with a glorious taste of potato that is not spoilt by rivulets of grease. They make fabulous snacks and nibbles, or a first course, especially when dipped into a tangy sauce.

INGREDIENTS

2 or 3 baking potatoes, each about 180g (6oz), scrubbed

oil-water spray (see page 29)

salt

1 Pat the potatoes dry with kitchen paper and cut into wedges, sticks or slices.

2 Oil-water spray a non-stick baking sheet and arrange the potato pieces, well-spaced, on it. Roast in a preheated oven for about 10 minutes.

3 Take the baking sheet from the oven, shake up the potatoes and turn them over. Return them to the oven and bake for another 15 minutes or so, until the potatoes are golden brown and puffed up. Salt them lightly and serve to great acclaim.

VARIATIONS

Oven-fried New Potatoes: scrub 500g (1lb) new potatoes, cut in half and bake as in the main recipe. New potatoes may take a little longer, perhaps 15 minutes on the first side, 20 minutes on the second side.

Spicy Oven-fries: for 500g (1lb) of cubed all-purpose potatoes or peeled and cubed sweet potatoes, stir a few drops of lemon or lime juice into 1½ tablespoons tomato purée. Add about 1½ teaspoons spice mixture – perhaps an Indian mixture, such as turmeric, garam masala, cumin and coriander; or a Mexican one, such as paprika and chilli powder; or simply a good curry powder. Toss the potato cubes in the mixture and bake as in the main recipe, turning the potato cubes several times.

Per serving

Total fat (g)	<1
Saturated fat (g)	neg
Unsaturated fat (g)	<1
Cholesterol (mg)	0
Sodium (mg)	105
Calories	87

 Oven temperature
220°C/425°F/gas 7

 Cooking time
About 25 minutes

Makes
4 servings

GARLIC MASHED POTATOES

To make the creamiest, richest-tasting no-fat mashed potatoes imaginable, start with very well baked (not boiled) potatoes. Then just follow my recipe.

INGREDIENTS

3 baking potatoes, each about 300g (10oz), scrubbed

9–12 roasted or pan-braised garlic cloves (see pages 35 and 78)

3–4 tbsp warm stock (see page 30)

3–4 tbsp warm skimmed milk

salt and freshly ground black pepper

snipped fresh chives, optional

1 Pierce the potatoes in several places with a fork or skewer and set them on a rack in the centre of a preheated oven. Bake for about 2 hours.

2 Hold the potatoes with an oven glove and pierce an X on the top of each with a fork.

Squeeze so that the flesh comes surging up through the crisp skin. Scoop the flesh into a bowl and mash with a fork. (Save the crunchy skins for a snack.)

3 Add the garlic cloves and mash thoroughly. Mix in the stock and milk, a tablespoon of each at a time, until the preferred texture is achieved. Season and then stir in chives, if desired.

VARIATION

Garlic-Parmesan Mashed Potatoes: follow the main recipe, but replace the stock and milk with 1–2 tablespoons very low-fat fromage frais and 2–3 tablespoons grated Parmesan cheese.

Per serving

Total fat (g)	<1
Saturated fat (g)	neg
Unsaturated fat (g)	<1
Cholesterol (mg)	neg
Sodium (mg)	28
Calories	110

 Oven temperature
200°C/400°F/gas 6

 Cooking time
About 2 hours

 Makes
4 servings

SWEET POTATO PANCAKES

This is a very turn-of-the-twentieth-century recipe. The colour is tropical orange, the texture is tender with crispy edges, and the seasoning is a Mexican-Caribbean blend. Serve these as a first course or light meal with a mango salsa, or accompanied by Borlotti Bean & Parma Ham Stew (see page 116). They are also good with Braised Chicken Mexican (see page 87).

INGREDIENTS

2 egg whites

½ tsp each ground ginger, ground coriander, turmeric, ground cumin and paprika

¼ tsp ground cinnamon

several dashes of Tabasco sauce

salt and freshly ground black pepper

2 tbsp lemon juice

1 large red onion

500g (1lb) orange-fleshed sweet potatoes, peeled

60g (2oz) flour

oil-water spray (see page 29)

1 Lightly beat the egg whites in a large bowl. Whisk in the spices, Tabasco, salt, pepper and lemon juice. Set aside.

2 Coarsely grate the onion into a colander, then grate the sweet potato over the onion. Whisk the flour into the egg mixture. With your hands, squeeze the grated potato and onion to get rid of excess liquid, then add to the egg mixture. Toss together gently until well mixed.

3 Oil-spray two non-stick baking trays and warm them in a preheated oven. Use a large spoon to scoop dollops of potato mixture on to the trays. Flatten each mound with the back of a spoon then moisten with oil-water spray.

4 Bake for 7–10 minutes. Turn, and spray again. Bake for 5–7 minutes more, then turn. Repeat once or twice until tender, with crisp brown edges. Serve hot, with lime wedges, if liked.

VARIATION

White Potato Pancakes: replace the sweet potato with white potatoes. Omit the spices. Add a pinch of nutmeg and a generous sprinkling of snipped chives. Garnish with fromage frais mixed with chopped chives and horseradish, and perhaps a little shredded smoked salmon.

 Per serving

Total fat (g)	1
Saturated fat (g)	neg
Unsaturated fat (g)	1
Cholesterol (mg)	0
Sodium (mg)	67
Calories	126

 Oven temperature
230°C/450°F/gas 8

 Baking time
About 25–30 minutes

 Makes
6 servings

SAUTE POTATOES WITH LEMON & MINT

These potatoes are resonant with lemon and are perfect with any pan-sautéed or roasted meat or poultry. I love their deep flavour – it doesn't just sit on top of the potatoes, it permeates them. The torn mint leaves complement them perfectly.

INGREDIENTS

500g (1lb) small new potatoes, scrubbed and halved lengthways

300ml (½ pint) stock (see page 30), plus a little extra (see method)

4 tbsp freshly squeezed lemon juice

several dashes of Tabasco sauce

salt and freshly ground black pepper

handful of torn mint leaves, to garnish

1 Put the potatoes, stock, 2 tablespoons of lemon juice, and the Tabasco in a heavy-based, non-stick frying pan. Season with salt and pepper. Bring to the boil, then cover and simmer briskly for 5–7 minutes. Uncover and simmer, stirring occasionally, until the potatoes are very tender, and the liquid has reduced. Do not let them burn: add a little more stock, if necessary.

2 When the potatoes are tender and the liquid has evaporated, stir the mixture and cook for a minute or so more, until the potatoes are lightly toasted and speckled with brown. Sprinkle with the remaining lemon juice and scatter over the mint leaves.

 Per serving

Total fat (g)	<1
Saturated fat (g)	neg
Unsaturated fat (g)	<1
Cholesterol (mg)	0
Sodium (mg)	88.5
Calories	102

 Makes
4 servings

GARLIC & LEMON ROASTED POTATOES

These potatoes are perfect with Lemon-Garlic Roasted Chicken (see page 84). Both offer no compromise in flavour, although they are very low-fat. The potatoes absorb the flavours of the added ingredients: "moreish" doesn't begin to describe them. Illustrated opposite.

INGREDIENTS

750g (1½lb) small waxy, oval potatoes, scrubbed but unpeeled

2 tbsp lemon juice

1 large, firm head of garlic, split into separate cloves

4 sun-dried tomatoes, quartered

4 black olives, slivered off their stones

4–5 dashes of Tabasco sauce

dash of Worcestershire sauce

dash of Teriyaki sauce

4 tbsp stock (see page 30), plus extra (see method)

oil-water spray (see page 29)

chopped fresh parsley, to garnish

1 Cut the potatoes into halves lengthways and spread them out in a shallow roasting tin with the remaining ingredients, except the oil-water spray and the chopped parsley.

2 Mist with oil-water spray, then transfer to a preheated oven and roast for approximately 30 minutes, stirring occasionally and adding small measures of stock as needed to prevent the potatoes burning.

3 When the potatoes are tender, speckled with charred patches, and the pan juices are thick and syrupy, remove from the oven, sprinkle them with chopped parsley, and serve.

VARIATION

This recipe is also delicious made with small whole new potatoes. Each tiny potato makes a succulent mouthful. Cooking time may be a little less.

 Per serving

Total fat (g)	<1
Saturated fat (g)	neg
Unsaturated fat (g)	<1
Cholesterol (mg)	0
Sodium (mg)	77
Calories	106

 Oven temperature
200°C/400°F/gas 6

 Cooking time
About 30 minutes

Makes
4 servings

MUSHROOMS MADE WILD

The "holy trinity" of fat-free mushroom cookery – stock, wine and Teriyaki sauce – brings out the mushroom flavour like nothing else. Add other flavour infusion ingredients and dried porcini, and your supermarket mushrooms will taste as if they were gathered in the woods at dawn. Illustrated on pages 113 and 151.

INGREDIENTS

4 garlic cloves, crushed

4 black olives, slivered off their stones

4 sun-dried tomatoes, chopped

1 chilli, deseeded and finely chopped

125ml (4fl oz) dry red wine

250ml (8fl oz) mushroom soaking stock (see page 30)

500g (1lb) closed-cup button mushrooms

30g (1oz) dried porcini, soaked, rinsed, drained and chopped

dash of Teriyaki or soy sauce

1 Put the garlic, olives, sun-dried tomatoes, chilli, wine, and half the stock in a heavy-based, flat-bottomed wok or frying pan. Bring to the boil and continue to boil until the liquid is reduced to about 1 tablespoon.

2 Add the button mushrooms, the remaining mushroom stock, the rehydrated porcini and the Teriyaki or soy sauce to the pan.

3 Reduce the heat and simmer briskly, uncovered. Stir occasionally, until the mushrooms are tender and coated in the reduced sauce.

4 Serve the mushrooms heaped on grilled polenta squares (see page 112). They also make a delicious accompaniment to pork dishes.

 Per serving

Total fat (g)	1
Saturated fat (g)	neg
Unsaturated fat (g)	1
Cholesterol (mg)	0
Sodium (mg)	86
Calories	51

 Makes
4 servings

ARTICHOKES WITH A HERBED OLIVE STUFFING

Artichokes stuffed with a savoury bread mixture make a beautiful first course, served hot or cold, or part of an antipasti platter. When serving whole artichokes, dechoke the heart first, so that feasting on the stuffed thistle will be easy and stress-free. If you do not have artichoke stock to hand, vegetable stock will do nicely.

INGREDIENTS

6 artichokes, prepared to end of step 2 of Preparing Artichokes, opposite

125ml (4fl oz) artichoke stock (see below), plus extra (see method)

For the stuffing

2–3 large garlic cloves, crushed

1 tbsp balsamic vinegar

juice of ½ lemon

6 tbsp chopped fresh parsley

3 tbsp chopped fresh mint

60g (2oz) day-old white bread

4–5 olives, slivered off their stones

1 tsp olive brine

freshly ground black pepper

3 tbsp artichoke stock

oil-water spray (see page 29)

1 Spread the artichokes' outer leaves apart, remove the cone of purplish leaves inside and use a teaspoon to scrape out all the inedible hairy choke. Pour the stock into a shallow baking dish. Arrange the artichokes in one layer in the dish.

2 For the stuffing, put the garlic, vinegar and lemon juice in a bowl, and leave to marinate for 10 minutes.

3 Mix the parsley, mint, shredded bread, olives and olive brine together. Stir in the garlic mixture and grind over black pepper to taste. Sprinkle in the artichoke stock and mix everything together well.

4 Push a generous amount of stuffing into the centre of each artichoke, slipping some of the stuffing down between the leaves. Sprinkle stock over each artichoke, then mist each one lightly with oil-water spray.

5 Loosely cover the artichokes with foil, and bake in a preheated oven for 15 minutes. Remove the cover. If the stuffing looks dry, sprinkle with a little more stock and mist again with oil-water spray.

6 Return the artichokes to the oven for 10–15 minutes. Check for tenderness by piercing the bottom of an artichoke with the point of a knife. If it seems hard, return to the oven and bake for a few minutes longer.

VARIATIONS

Stuffed Artichoke Hearts: take 6 artichoke hearts (see Preparing Artichokes, opposite), and press about a tablespoon of the stuffing (above) on each. Arrange them in a single layer in a baking dish. Tuck the remaining stuffing over and around. Pour stock into the dish to a depth of 2.5cm (1in). Cover with foil and bake for 20–25 minutes. Uncover and sprinkle over 3 tablespoons Parmesan. Re-cover and bake for 20 minutes. Serve at once.

Artichokes with Vinaigrette: serve whole artichokes with Basic Vinaigrette (see page 59).

NOTE

Artichoke leaves make a vivid, intense stock. Put in a large pan with plenty of cold water. Bring to the boil, then cover and simmer for about 45 minutes. Drain through a colander into a pan, then press down on the leaves to extract more liquid. Leave to cool, then pour into small containers and freeze. Artichoke stock makes a good base for soup, and is an excellent sauté medium.

Per serving	
Total fat (g)	1
Saturated fat (g)	neg
Unsaturated fat (g)	1
Cholesterol (mg)	0
Sodium (mg)	161
Calories	68

Oven temperature
180°C/350°F/gas 4

Cooking time
25–30 minutes

Makes
6 servings

ARTICHOKE & COURGETTE STIR-FRY

This stir-fry makes a vibrant first course, a light lunch or a colourful accompaniment to fish or poultry, for example grilled chicken breasts.

INGREDIENTS

6 baby courgettes

6 artichoke hearts (see Preparing Artichokes, below)

8 stalks asparagus

1 large red pepper

1 large yellow pepper

oil-water spray (see page 29)

approximately 125ml (4fl oz) artichoke stock (see opposite) or other stock (see page 30)

salt and freshly ground black pepper

juice of ½ lime or lemon, to taste

1 Using a sharp knife, trim the courgettes and halve them lengthways. Cut the artichoke hearts into strips.

2 Trim and peel the asparagus stalks, then cut them crossways into 2.5cm (1in) lengths.

3 Peel the peppers (see page 34), halve, core and deseed them and cut them into strips.

4 Spray a non-stick, flat-bottomed wok with oil-water spray. Put the courgette halves, artichoke strips, asparagus, and pepper strips into the wok.

5 Pour in the stock, and season with salt and freshly ground black pepper.

6 Sauté over a high heat, constantly stirring and turning the vegetables, until they are crisp but tender and the stock has reduced. Sprinkle over the lime or lemon juice.

7 Serve the stir-fry immediately, perhaps with slices of Wild Mushroom Bread (see page 146).

VARIATION

To make this a more substantial, non-vegetarian main dish, add slices of Smoked Spice-rubbed Duck Breasts (see page 90), or serve it with Crusty "Grill-fried" Pork Escalopes (see page 95).

Per serving

Total fat (g)	1
Saturated fat (g)	neg
Unsaturated fat (g)	<1
Cholesterol (mg)	0
Sodium (mg)	14
Calories	80

Makes
6 servings

PREPARING ARTICHOKES

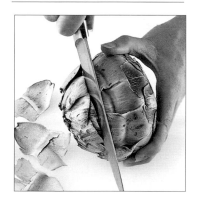

1 Cut or break off the stem of each artichoke, trim the base and slice 2.5cm (1in) off the top. As soon as it is trimmed, drop each artichoke into a bowl of water acidulated with the juice of 1 lemon to prevent discoloration.

2 Snap off the artichokes' tough outer leaves. Put the whole artichokes into a pan of lightly salted boiling water and boil, partially covered, for 25–30 minutes. Drain, rinse under cold running water and drain again, upside down.

3 To prepare artichoke hearts, pull off all the remaining leaves, reserving them for stock (see opposite). Pull out the purplish leaves over the heart. Using a paring knife and a teaspoon, scrape out all the inedible hairy choke.

4 When all vestiges of the inedible choke have been removed, trim off the artichoke's hard base, leaving just the tender artichoke heart. It is now ready for stuffing and baking, or for using in dishes like the stir-fry above.

FENNEL

Fennel, the whole vegetable or its seeds, gives its anise blessing to several recipes in this book. Always trim the bulbs as described here before using in the chosen recipe.

To prepare whole fennel bulbs for cooking, trim away the tough outer layer, and cut off the stalks and leaves from the head of the fennel bulb. (Save the trimmings for stock-making and save the feathery fronds to use as a herb garnish.) Trim the bottom of the bulb slightly, but leave the core intact, as it helps to keep the fennel sections together as they cook.

Per 500g (1lb)	
Total fat (g)	1
Saturated fat (g)	neg
Unsaturated fat (g)	1
Cholesterol (mg)	0
Sodium (mg)	55
Calories	60

OVEN-ROASTED BEETROOT

Acrid, flabby beetroot, overcooked and "preserved" with bad vinegar, debases the superb scarlet roots. Buy beetroot fresh, oven-roast it and taste the difference.

Choose beetroots of a similar size, if possible. Wrap the prepared beetroot in heavy-duty foil (shiny side in). With smaller beetroot, put 2–3 in a packet. Wrap them so that the beetroots are in roomy, well sealed packets. Bake at 200°C/400°F/gas 6 for 1–2 hours (the timing depends on the age and size of the roots). Use a skewer to test if the beetroots are tender. The skewer should go in easily, but the roots should not be mushy. Also, the skins will give slightly when pressed. Cool slightly, then slip off the skins.

Per 500g (1lb)	
Total fat (g)	<1
Saturated fat (g)	neg
Unsaturated fat (g)	<1
Cholesterol (mg)	0
Sodium (mg)	330
Calories	180

ASPARAGUS

Thick stalks of asparagus must be peeled, or they will turn fibrous when cooked. Always cook them briefly: limp asparagus stalks are a scandal!

Unless the asparagus stalks are pencil thin, peel them first to get maximum taste and texture out of the vegetable. Cut off the woody bottom of each stalk and use a swivel-bladed vegetable peeler to peel the stalk from the bottom end up to the bud. Rinse the stalks under cold running water and, if you are not going to use them at once, stand them in a glass of water as if they were a bunch of flowers, cover with a plastic bag and keep in the refrigerator until needed.

To cook, put the stalks in a steamer basket and steam over boiling water for 3-7 minutes, depending on their size, until they are just tender. They should retain a hint of crispness. To test, hold up a stalk with tongs: it should bend just a little bit. If you intend serving the asparagus hot, drain it on a clean tea towel, set on a rack. If you plan to serve it cold, refresh it under cold running water to stop the cooking process and to set its bright green colour. Drain and cool.

Per 500g (1lb)	
Total fat (g)	3
Saturated fat (g)	1
Unsaturated fat (g)	2
Cholesterol (mg)	0
Sodium (mg)	5
Calories	125

PAN-BRAISED GARLIC

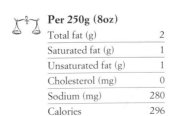

Per 250g (8oz)	
Total fat (g)	2
Saturated fat (g)	1
Unsaturated fat (g)	1
Cholesterol (mg)	0
Sodium (mg)	280
Calories	296

Peel any number of garlic cloves (see page 35). Spread the garlic cloves in a heavy-based frying pan and cover generously with stock. Cover tightly and simmer for 10–15 minutes, until the garlic cloves are meltingly tender and the stock is greatly reduced. (You may need to check and top-up the stock during cooking.) Drain the garlic (keep any leftover stock for soups or sauces) and purée, either by mashing it or pushing it through a fine-mesh nylon sieve.

AUBERGINE & TOMATO GRATIN

Cooked in the traditional way, aubergine soaks up oil like an insatiable sponge. Save hundreds (maybe thousands!) of calories by grilling aubergine with a spritz of oil-water spray instead. As a result, this low-fat version of a beloved Italian home-cooking favourite will be ephemeral rather than stodgy.

INGREDIENTS

10 heaped tbsp fresh white breadcrumbs

5 tbsp freshly grated Parmesan cheese

salt and freshly ground black pepper

2 tbsp plain flour

3 egg whites

2–3 dashes of Tabasco sauce

two 250g (8oz) aubergines, trimmed and peeled (see page 36)

oil-water spray (see page 29)

½ quantity Tomato, Garlic & Pepper Sauce (see page 64)

1 Put the breadcrumbs in a shallow bowl with 3 tablespoons of Parmesan cheese. Season with salt and pepper.

2 Put the flour in another shallow bowl, and season lightly with salt and pepper.

3 Put the egg whites in another shallow bowl and season with salt, pepper and Tabasco. Beat lightly with a fork.

4 Preheat the grill. Slice the aubergines on the diagonal, then dredge in the seasoned flour. Dip the slices on both sides into the egg whites and breadcrumbs, then dip again in the egg and crumbs. Transfer the pieces to a platter as you work.

5 Spray a non-stick baking sheet with oil-water spray and place under the grill to heat. Put the aubergine slices on the hot sheet, and spray the tops.

6 Put under the hot grill and grill, 10cm (4in) from the heat, for about 5 minutes, or until browned and sizzling. Loosen the slices carefully, turn, oil-spray and grill on the second side for another 5 minutes, or until browned and tender. Meanwhile, heat the Tomato, Garlic & Pepper Sauce.

7 Lay the aubergine slices in a gratin dish and pour the sauce over the top. Sprinkle with the remaining Parmesan and flash under the grill until bubbly.

Per serving

Total fat (g)	6
Saturated fat (g)	3
Unsaturated fat (g)	3
Cholesterol (mg)	13
Sodium (mg)	403
Calories	208

Makes
6 servings

RICOTTA PARMESAN CUSTARD

This savoury custard makes an exciting topping for Lasagne (see pages 110 and 111), and for vegetable dishes. For example, the Aubergine & Tomato Gratin (see page 79) can be topped with the custard instead of the Parmesan.

INGREDIENTS

3 egg whites

250g (8oz) ricotta cheese

175ml (6fl oz) skimmed milk

5 tbsp freshly grated Parmesan

salt and freshly ground black pepper

1 Beat the egg whites with the ricotta, then beat in the milk and 4 tablespoons of Parmesan.

Season with salt and pepper. Pour the mixture over the chosen recipe, tilting the baking dish to produce an even coating.

2 Sprinkle the remaining Parmesan over the custard. Transfer to an oven preheated to 180°C/350°F/gas 4. Bake for 30 – 40 minutes, until softly set and puffed and golden. Allow to sit for 5 minutes before serving.

Per serving

Total fat (g)	9
Saturated fat (g)	6
Unsaturated fat (g)	3
Cholesterol (mg)	34
Sodium (mg)	222
Calories	132

 Makes
6 servings

BREADED AUBERGINE & COURGETTE SLICES

Serve these grill-"fried" vegetables (they look endearingly like fried fish) with Tomato, Garlic & Pepper Sauce (see page 64). They would also be good with a salsa from the Sauces & Salsas section, or with Basic Vinaigrette (see page 59) served as a dipping sauce.

INGREDIENTS

500g (1lb) very low-fat natural yogurt

1 red or yellow pepper, grilled, skinned (see page 35) and puréed

1½ tsp Dijon mustard

5–6 tbsp fresh soft breadcrumbs, from white or brown bread

4–5 tbsp freshly grated Parmesan

pinch or two of paprika

salt and freshly ground black pepper

1 aubergine, about 250g (8oz), peeled and trimmed (see page 36)

1 courgette, about 180g (6oz), trimmed

oil-water spray (see page 29)

lemon wedges, to garnish

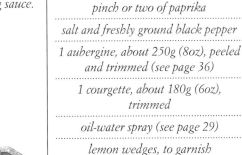

1 Put the yogurt in a bowl, and gently whisk in the pepper purée and mustard. Pour on to a large plate and spread evenly.

2 Put the breadcrumbs on another large plate, mix in the grated Parmesan and paprika and season with salt and pepper. Spread the mixture out evenly.

3 Cut the aubergine and courgette lengthways into slices about 5mm (¼in) thick. Coat each

slice in the yogurt mixture, then dredge them in breadcrumbs, pressing them on firmly.

4 Spray a non-stick baking sheet with oil-water spray and place it under a grill to heat. When it is hot, take out from under the grill and carefully spray again.

5 Arrange the aubergine and courgette slices (in batches if necessary) on the sheet, leaving space around each slice. Place 12cm (5in) below the grill and cook for 3–5 minutes.

6 Remove the baking sheet from the heat and turn the slices over. Mist with the oil-water spray and put back under the grill until the reversed sides are browned and sizzling and the vegetable slices are very tender (check with the point of a knife or a skewer).

7 Transfer the cooked vegetable slices to a warm platter and keep warm while you grill the remaining vegetable slices.

8 Garnish the platter with lemon wedges and serve at once, with your chosen sauce or salsa in a separate bowl.

Per serving

Total fat (g)	8
Saturated fat (g)	4
Unsaturated fat (g)	3
Cholesterol (mg)	22
Sodium (mg)	494
Calories	259

 **Makes**
4 servings

GRILLED AUBERGINES & COURGETTES

The technique of twice-cooking courgette and aubergine slices, first in an oil-water sprayed frying pan, and then in a ridged grill pan, ensures that the vegetables are meltingly tender with an elusive sweet and smoky barbecue flavour. I like to serve these as part of an antipasto, piled on to a platter with lemon wedges. They also make a wonderful filling for lasagne or for sandwiches.

INGREDIENTS

oil-water spray (see page 29)

1 long aubergine, about 250g (8oz), peeled and trimmed (see page 36)

2 tender young courgettes, about 125g (4oz) each, trimmed

1 Spray a heavy-based non-stick pan with oil-water spray and set it and a ridged grill pan over a medium heat to warm through.

2 Meanwhile, slice the aubergine and courgettes lengthways into 5mm (¼in) thick slices. Place the slices, in batches, in the non-stick pan, leaving space around each slice. Cook for a minute or two on each side until tender and just beginning to show brown speckles, misting with the oil-water spray after turning.

3 Remove the pan from the heat and immediately transfer the slices in batches to the grill pan, keeping them well spaced. Grill for a minute or so on each side without spraying until marked by the grill.

4 Transfer each batch to a warm platter and keep warm while you grill the remaining slices.

Per serving

Total fat (g)	1
Saturated fat (g)	neg
Unsaturated fat (g)	1
Cholesterol (mg)	0
Sodium (mg)	2
Calories	23

Makes
4 servings

SPICED GREEN BEANS WITH LIME

An Asian-inspired treatment for tiny green beans. This dish is good hot, cold or at room temperature. Use as an accompaniment to fish or Tandoori-style Chicken (see page 86).

INGREDIENTS

juice of ½ lime

300ml (½ pint) stock (see page 30)

½–1 chilli, deseeded and finely chopped

½ tsp ground turmeric

½ tsp ground coriander

pinch of sugar

2 garlic cloves, crushed

1cm (½in) piece of root ginger, crushed

500g (1lb) dwarf green beans, trimmed

salt and freshly ground black pepper

1 Mix together the lime juice, half the stock, chilli, spices, sugar, garlic and ginger in a wok and simmer over a high heat until almost all the liquid has evaporated.

2 Add the beans and the remaining stock and season with salt and pepper. Cover and simmer for 3–5 minutes. Uncover and simmer briskly for 2 minutes more, stirring continuously, until just tender – the beans should remain bright green and slightly crunchy.

Per serving

Total fat (g)	<1
Saturated fat (g)	neg
Unsaturated fat (g)	<1
Cholesterol (mg)	0
Sodium (mg)	67.5
Calories	45

Makes
4 servings

POULTRY

CHICKEN BREAST FILLETS, without bones and skin, are delicate, low-fat morsels, but, alas, boringly bland. A whole roasted bird, minus its skin, fat and the usual oily or buttery baste, can suffer the same insipid fate. Zap breast fillets with plenty of assertive herbs and spices, baste them in citrus juices and vegetable purée sauces, surround them with heady collections of vegetables and they will take on deep character. Duck breasts and chicken thighs, stripped of skin and fat, are more robust in flavour, but also benefit from bold seasoning. Cook chicken thoroughly, but don't overcook it: *over*-cooked means dry and stringy.

CHICKEN WITH MEDITERRANEAN VEGETABLES
looks beautiful served on a platter with lemon wedges and a lavish garnishing of fresh herbs.

MAKING A FLAVOUR INFUSION

The flavour infusion for this dish is based on vegetables with a Mediterranean slant, including olives, peppers and sun-dried tomatoes.

RED ONION

GARLIC CLOVES

SUN-DRIED TOMATO

BLACK OLIVES

AUBERGINE

RED AND YELLOW PEPPERS   RED CHILLI

DRY WHITE WINE

CHICKEN STOCK

CAPERS

RAISINS

CHICKEN WITH MEDITERRANEAN VEGETABLES

INGREDIENTS

4 chicken breast fillets, trimmed

For the marinade

4 garlic cloves, crushed

2 olives, slivered off their stones

juice of 1 large orange

90ml (3fl oz) lemon juice

2 tbsp balsamic vinegar

2 dashes of Teriyaki sauce

For the vegetable flavour infusion

1 large red onion, halved and sliced

4 garlic cloves, crushed

4 sun-dried tomatoes, chopped

4 black olives, slivered off their stones

1 red chilli, deseeded and chopped

180g (6oz) aubergine, peeled and diced (see page 36)

2 tbsp each raisins and capers

1 red and 1 yellow pepper, deseeded, peeled and cut into strips (see page 34)

300ml (½ pint) stock (see page 30)

300ml (½ pint) dry white wine

salt and freshly ground black pepper

oil-water spray (see page 29)

1 Put the skinned chicken fillets in a dish. Mix the marinade ingredients and pour over the chicken. Leave to marinate.

2 Heat the flavour infusion ingredients in a frying pan, cover and simmer for 5–7 minutes. Uncover and simmer until the vegetables are tender.

3 Heat a ridged grill pan; spray with oil-water spray. Shake the marinade off the chicken and grill for 2–3 minutes on each side.

4 Lay the chicken in one layer on the vegetables in the pan, cover and simmer gently, turning, for 7–8 minutes until cooked. Serve garnished with fresh herbs, if liked.

Per serving

Total fat (g)	3
Saturated fat (g)	1
Unsaturated fat (g)	2
Cholesterol (mg)	84
Sodium (mg)	290
Calories	271

Makes
4 servings

LEMON GARLIC ROASTED CHICKEN

I really feel that this is the ultimate roasted chicken. It proves triumphantly that very low-fat cooking does not mean compromising on flavour. Serve the succulent bird and its delicious natural gravy with Garlic and Lemon Roasted Potatoes. As with all chicken recipes, while the bird should be at room temperature when it goes into the oven, to ensure even cooking right through, never leave it sitting in a warm atmosphere before cooking it.

INGREDIENTS

1 large head garlic (about 14 large cloves), separated

4 sun-dried tomatoes, halved lengthways, and 1 sun-dried tomato, chopped

4 black olives, slivered off their stones

500ml (16fl oz) stock (see page 30)

several dashes of Tabasco sauce

1–2 dashes each of Teriyaki and Worcestershire sauces

one 1.25–1.5kg (2½–3lb) chicken, trimmed of all fat

90ml (3fl oz) lemon juice (lemon halves reserved)

1 lemon, thinly sliced and pips removed

1 large onion, sliced

about 175ml (6fl oz) dry vermouth

salt and freshly ground black pepper

125–175ml (4–6fl oz) dry white vermouth (for the gravy)

1 large bunch watercress, to garnish

1 Lightly crush 12 garlic cloves to loosen the skins. Remove the skins and halve each clove. Remove any central green sprouts.

2 Put the halved garlic into a frying pan with the sun-dried tomato halves, olives, 300ml (½ pint) stock, Tabasco, Teriyaki and Worcestershire sauces. Simmer briskly until the garlic is very tender and the liquid is greatly reduced and syrupy. Allow to cool.

3 Make small incisions all over the chicken (except the breast). Rub lemon juice over the bird. Loosen the breast skin and rub lemon juice under the skin. Put the lemon halves into the main cavity.

4 Spread the lemon slices and garlic mixture evenly under the breast skin. Transfer to a glass or ceramic dish, cover and chill for several hours or overnight.

5 Take the bird out of the refrigerator and tie its legs together. Scatter the onion, remaining garlic, chopped, and chopped sun-dried tomato in a roasting tin. Put a rack in the tin.

6 Pour 60ml (2fl oz) each of stock and vermouth in the tin. Season the chicken, and roast it breast down on the rack for 30 minutes, then breast up for about 40 minutes.

7 Add stock and vermouth as needed to keep the juices plentiful, and baste the chicken occasionally. Turn it regularly to stop it over-browning. It is done when golden brown and the juices run clear when the leg joint is pricked. Let rest for 10 minutes, then take off all the skin and the flavour ingredients underneath it.

SERVING THE CHICKEN

1 For the gravy, pour the pan juices through a sieve into a bowl. Press down on the solids to squeeze out all the goodness. Discard the solids. Freeze the pan juices for 10 minutes, so that the fat can rise to the top and solidify.

2 Put the roasting tin on the hob, pour in the white vermouth, and reduce the liquid by half, scraping up the browned deposits. Skim the fat from the chilled pan juices, pour the juices into the roasting tin and bring to the boil. Pour into a warmed jug.

3 Garnish the carved chicken with watercress and serve with the gravy and Garlic and Lemon Roasted Potatoes (see page 74).

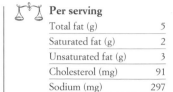

Per serving

Total fat (g)	5
Saturated fat (g)	2
Unsaturated fat (g)	3
Cholesterol (mg)	91
Sodium (mg)	297
Calories	211

Oven temperature
230°C/450°F/gas 8

Cooking time
About 1½ hours

Makes
4 servings

84

SMOKED ROSEMARY LEMON POUSSINS

In low-fat cooking, flavour is all. Cross-cultural French/Chinese overtones – a rosemary-garlic-olive-lemon mixture stuffed under the skin and tea, sugar and rice in the wok for smoking – imbue these birds with fabulous flavour. The poussins are wok-smoked first then oven-roasted. The roasting time depends on the force of the heat under the wok during the initial smoking, so treat the final roasting times given here as a guide only.

INGREDIENTS

2 poussins, each about 425g (14oz), fat trimmed

4 garlic cloves

6 black olives, slivered off their stones

4 tbsp fresh rosemary needles, plus 2 long sprigs

juice of 2 lemons

mixed peppercorns

3 rounded tbsp Lapsang Souchong tea or the contents of 6 teabags

3 rounded tbsp brown sugar

3 rounded tbsp white rice

salt

oil-water spray (see page 29)

1 Loosen the skin over the poussin breasts and legs by running your finger between the skin and the flesh.

2 Crush together the garlic and olives and mix with the rosemary needles and half the lemon juice. Slip this mixture under the skin of the poussins, pushing it over the breasts, and down to the legs. Sprinkle the remaining lemon juice over the birds, and grind over the peppercorns. Cover and leave to marinate in the refrigerator for several hours or overnight.

3 Take a wok with a tight fitting lid and line it with aluminium foil, leaving an overhang around the edge (see Smoked Spice-rubbed Duck Breasts, page 90).

4 Spoon the tea, sugar and rice on to the aluminium foil, then cut up the rosemary sprigs and add them as well. Put a steaming rack into the wok.

5 Season the poussins with salt, then arrange them, breast down, on the steaming rack, and cover the wok. Crimp the foil around the lid to prevent smoke from escaping. Turn the heat to high for 5 minutes, then cook on low for another 20 minutes. Meanwhile, preheat the oven and line a baking sheet with foil, shiny side up. Place a rack on the sheet.

6 Spray the rack with oil-water spray. Put the smoked poussins, breast up, on the rack, and roast in the preheated oven for 10 minutes. Turn breast down and roast for 10 minutes. Finally, turn breast up again and cook for 5 minutes. Remove from the oven and leave to rest for 5 minutes.

7 To serve, strip off and discard the poussin skin and the herb-garlic mixture, which will have permeated the flesh. Carve the poussins, and serve the pieces on warm plates. Alternatively, present each diner with half a bird, and let them tackle it (it's less elegant, but more rewarding).

 Per serving

Total fat (g)	4
Saturated fat (g)	1
Unsaturated fat (g)	3
Cholesterol (mg)	61
Sodium (mg)	181
Calories	238

 Oven temperature
230°C/450°F/gas 8

Cooking time
50 minutes

Makes
4 servings

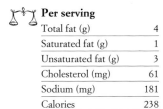

TANDOORI-STYLE CHICKEN

Without a conical clay tandoor oven, there is no true tandoori chicken, so this is an approximation only – but a delicious one. A combination of grilling and roasting gives the right effect here.

INGREDIENTS

4 chicken breasts, skinned and trimmed

salt and freshly ground black pepper

1 tbsp each ground coriander and ground cumin

1 tsp each ground turmeric and garam masala

¼ tsp each freshly grated nutmeg, ground cinnamon, chilli powder and ground cardamom

pinch of ground cloves

350ml (12fl oz) very low-fat yogurt

6 garlic cloves, crushed

2.5cm (1in) piece of fresh root ginger, peeled and crushed

oil-water spray (see page 29)

chopped fresh coriander leaves, to garnish

1 Pull the thin, goujon-size fillet from each chicken breast. Pierce each piece of chicken in several places with a thin skewer. Season with salt and pepper.

2 Mix the remaining ingredients except the oil-water spray and garnish. Toss the chicken in this mixture and spread out the pieces in a ceramic or glass baking dish.

Cover tightly with clingfilm and chill in the refrigerator for several hours or overnight.

3 Bring the chicken to room temperature. Oil-water spray a non-stick baking sheet and put it in the preheated oven.

4 Heat a ridged grill pan over the hob. When it is very hot, lay the chicken on the pan in a single layer. Grill for 1½–2 minutes on each side, turning occasionally, until the pieces are well seared and striped with characteristic barbecue hatchmarks.

5 Transfer the larger seared fillets to the baking sheet and cook in a preheated oven until just done, about 4–5 minutes, depending on size. They are done when they feel firm yet springy. The smaller goujon pieces will cook through on the grill pan in about 3–4 minutes.

6 Slice all the chicken pieces across the grain. Serve on a bed of fragrant rice, garnished with the coriander. Accompany with lime wedges, pickles, chutney and Herbed Raita (see page 52).

Per serving

Total fat (g)	3
Saturated fat (g)	1
Unsaturated fat (g)	2
Cholesterol (mg)	86
Sodium (mg)	151
Calories	170

Oven temperature
230°C/450°F/gas 8

Cooking time
about 7 minutes

Makes
4 servings

CHICKEN BREASTS WITH BRAISED PRUNES & SHALLOTS

*B*randy-saturated prunes simmered with fresh tarragon, garlic and shallots give chicken breasts great character. They give the chicken the deep, dark flavours I crave, and the colours are richly autumnal.

INGREDIENTS

4 chicken breast fillets, skinned and well trimmed

salt and freshly ground black pepper

125ml (4fl oz) dry white wine

2 tbsp brandy

125ml (4fl oz) stock (see page 30)

6 ready-to-eat prunes, stoned and quartered

oil–water spray (see page 29)

4 shallots, cut into eighths

2 garlic cloves, crushed

1½ tbsp chopped fresh tarragon

large bunch watercress, to garnish

1 Season each chicken breast fillet with a little salt and plenty of pepper. Put the wine, brandy, stock and prunes in a bowl or jug.

2 Spray a non-stick frying pan liberally with oil-water spray, and heat until it sizzles. Add the chicken breasts and brown for 1–2 minutes on each side. Set aside.

3 Pour the wine mixture into the frying pan, add the shallots, garlic and 1 tablespoon of tarragon and bring to the boil. Boil rapidly, deglazing the pan by scraping up the deposits on the bottom.

4 When the shallots are tender and the liquid greatly reduced, return the chicken to the pan with the remaining tarragon. Cook for 2–3 minutes only, turning the fillets, until they are mahogany brown and just cooked through. Add a splash of stock and wine, if needed, but remember that the sauce should be thick and syrupy.

5 Arrange the chicken on a warm platter with the prune-shallot mixture. Garnish with the watercress and serve.

Per serving

Total fat (g)	2
Saturated fat (g)	<1
Unsaturated fat (g)	1
Cholesterol (mg)	84
Sodium (mg)	104
Calories	178

Makes
4 servings

BRAISED CHICKEN MEXICAN

A Mexican-inspired dish in which the method of braising ensures that the seasoning infuses the chicken right down to the bone, and that the texture is deliciously succulent. Serve it with Sweet Potato Pancakes (see page 73), and Cherry Tomato & Red Onion Salsa (see page 61).

INGREDIENTS

3 garlic cloves, crushed

½ red and ½ green chilli, deseeded and chopped

12 spring onions, trimmed and sliced

juice of 1 lime

grated zest of ½ lime

½ tbsp ground cumin

½ tsp ground coriander

1 tbsp dark rum

1 tbsp tomato purée

salt and freshly ground black pepper

6 chicken thighs, skinned and trimmed

250ml (8fl oz) stock (see page 30)

chopped fresh coriander leaves, to garnish

1 Put all the ingredients in a bowl except the chicken, stock and coriander. Toss the chicken in this mixture and leave to marinate for up to 30 minutes.

2 Put the chicken thighs, with the marinade, in a single layer in a heavy-based frying pan. Pour in the stock.

3 Bring to a simmer. Continue to simmer for approximately 20 minutes, turning the chicken occasionally, until it is just done and the pan juices have cooked down to a thick, terracotta-coloured sauce.

4 Sprinkle over the coriander and serve with lime wedges.

Per serving

Total fat (g)	2
Saturated fat (g)	<1
Unsaturated fat (g)	1.5
Cholesterol (mg)	68
Sodium (mg)	125
Calories	97

Makes
4 servings

GRILLED CHICKEN WITH SWEET POTATO & LIME SAUCE

The sauce is a vivid blaze of yellow-orange and the chicken is exquisitely tender. The lime leaves used in the sauce are available in jars (freeze-dried) on the spice shelf in the supermarket. For a change, prepare the recipe to the middle of step 3, but leave the vegetable mixture unpuréed. Cube the grilled chicken and combine with the vegetables.

INGREDIENTS

juice of 1 lime

juice of ½ orange

½ tsp each turmeric, cumin and coriander

salt and freshly ground black pepper

4 boneless, skinless chicken breasts

For the sauce

2–3 garlic cloves, crushed

2.5cm (1in) piece of fresh root ginger, crushed

2 cardamom pods, lightly crushed

4 spring onions, sliced

½ tsp each cumin, turmeric and ground coriander

2 Kaffir lime leaves

500g (1lb) orange-fleshed sweet potato, peeled and diced

300ml (½ pint) stock (see page 30)

juice of ½ lime

few drops lemon juice

chopped fresh coriander, to garnish

1 Rub the juices, spices and salt and pepper into the chicken. Marinate while making the sauce.

2 To make the sauce, sauté the garlic, ginger, cardamom, spring onions, spices, lime leaves and sweet potato in a covered pan for 7–10 minutes. Uncover and cook for 3–5 minutes until the vegetables are tender. Discard the lime leaves and cardamom.

3 Add the stock, lime juice, lemon juice and salt and pepper. Process the mixture in a blender, then push through a sieve, discarding the solids.

4 Grill the chicken in a grill pan for 2–3 minutes, then finish in a preheated oven for 6–7 minutes. Reheat the sauce, taste, and adjust the seasoning. Spoon on to plates, put the chicken on the sauce and garnish with the coriander, and with spikes of chives, if liked.

Per serving

Total fat (g)	2
Saturated fat (g)	1
Unsaturated fat (g)	1
Cholesterol (mg)	84
Sodium (mg)	194
Calories	260

 Oven temperature
220°C/425°F/gas 7

 Cooking time
18–25 minutes

 Makes
4 servings

DUCK BREASTS WITH CRANBERRY CHUTNEY

The richness of duck breast is beautifully complemented by a sweet and sour chutney of plumped dried cranberries. The skinned duck – lean as can be – is cooked briefly so that it remains pink and succulent. Orange-Thyme Scented Wild Rice (see page 115) is the perfect accompaniment.

INGREDIENTS

4 boned duck breasts, skinned and trimmed of any fat

1 tbsp mixed peppercorns, crushed

oil-water spray (see page 29)

For the marinade

juice of ½ orange

4 tbsp lemon juice

½ tbsp balsamic vinegar

½ tbsp red vermouth

2 garlic cloves, crushed

1cm (½in) piece of fresh root ginger, crushed

¼ tsp each ground turmeric, ground cumin and ground coriander

For the chutney

1cm (½in) piece of fresh root ginger, crushed

2 garlic cloves, crushed

1 red onion, chopped

1 chilli, deseeded and chopped

juice of ½ orange

4 tbsp lemon juice, plus extra (see method)

150ml (¼ pint) stock (see page 30)

125ml (4fl oz) red vermouth

1 tbsp balsamic vinegar

75g (2½oz) dried cranberries

1 Coat the duck breasts on both sides with the crushed pepper, and place them in a single layer in a glass or ceramic dish.

2 Mix together the marinade ingredients, and pour the mixture over the duck. Turn the breasts in the liquid so that they are evenly coated. Leave to marinate at room temperature for 1–2 hours, or for several hours in the refrigerator. If refrigerated, let them come to room temperature before continuing.

3 Meanwhile, put the chutney ingredients in a saucepan, bring gently to the boil, and simmer until the onions are tender, the cranberries are plump, and the liquid is reduced to a syrupy glaze. Taste, and add a little more lemon juice if needed. Set aside.

4 Spread the chutney in a large flameproof, ovenproof frying pan large enough to hold the duck pieces in a single layer and bring to a simmer.

5 Meanwhile, oil-water spray a heavy-based non-stick frying pan and heat it on the hob. Sear the marinated duck breasts in the frying pan for about 1 minute on each side.

6 Set the duck on top of the chutney in a single layer and transfer the pan to a preheated oven. Roast for 7 minutes, until cooked, but still pink inside: the duck breasts should feel firm yet springy (not hard or mushy).

7 Set the duck on a chopping board and leave to rest for 5 minutes. Spread the chutney out on a serving plate. Slice the duck across the grain, and arrange the slices, overlapping slightly, on the chutney. Drizzle over any meat juices that have gathered under the duck breasts. Serve immediately.

Per serving

Total fat (g)	6
Saturated fat (g)	2
Unsaturated fat (g)	4
Cholesterol (mg)	132
Sodium (mg)	178
Calories	241

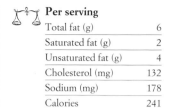

Oven temperature
200°C/400°F/gas 6

Oven cooking time
7 minutes

Makes
4 servings

SMOKED SPICE-RUBBED DUCK BREASTS

A long time ago, my friend, chef Frank Ma of Atlanta, Georgia, taught me how to smoke small pieces of poultry in a wok. It's a marvellous technique to apply to low-fat cooking, because the process leaves the poultry permeated with a haunting and compelling smokiness. Here I give three recipes using smoked duck breasts. Illustrated opposite is Duck and Pear Salad.

INGREDIENTS

3 rounded tbsp Lapsang Souchong tea, or the contents of 6 Lapsang Souchong tea bags

3 rounded tbsp white rice

3 rounded tbsp brown sugar

2–4 Barbary duck breasts, skinned and trimmed

good pinch or two each hot paprika, ground coriander and ground cumin

freshly ground black pepper

juice of 1 lime

oil-water spray (see page 29)

1 Take a wok with a tight-fitting lid and line it with aluminium foil, leaving an overhang. Sprinkle in the tea, rice and brown sugar. Put a steaming rack in the wok.

2 Put the duck breasts on a plate. Sprinkle the spices over and grind pepper evenly on both sides of the duck breasts and rub the mixture in. Squeeze the lime juice over them and turn the breasts in the juice.

3 Put the duck pieces on the steaming rack, and cover. Crimp the foil around the lid to keep the smoke in. Turn the heat to high for 5 minutes, then down to low for 5 minutes. Remove from the heat, and leave to sit, still covered, for 5 minutes more.

4 Oil-water spray a ridged grill pan and heat. Grill the duck breasts, turning once or twice, and oil-water spraying them briefly. They are best kept rare, and may take anywhere from 2 minutes to 6 or 7, depending on their size, the heat and your grill pan. Slice across the grain and serve with any pan juices.

VARIATION

Duck and Pear Salad: line a platter with watercress or rocket. Arrange on it slices of Smoked Duck Breasts, sliced pears, asparagus spears and fresh raspberries or blueberries. Drizzle over Pear Vinaigrette (see page 59) and sprinkle with fresh herbs.

Per serving

Total fat (g)	6
Saturated fat (g)	2
Unsaturated fat (g)	4
Cholesterol (mg)	132
Sodium (mg)	132
Calories	151

Makes
2 – 4 servings

SMOKED DUCK FAJITAS

This is a smoky, sensual, spicy, convivial glory of a feast, centred round the wonderful spiced and smoked duck breasts of the recipe above. No-one could feel glum sitting down to a meal like this.

INGREDIENTS

16–20 wheat tortillas

4 Smoked Spice-rubbed Duck Breasts (see above), sliced across the grain or cut into strips

selection of roasted vegetables, such as red and yellow peppers, courgettes and aubergines

Green Pea Guacamole (see page 50)

Cherry Tomato & Red Onion Salsa (see page 61)

Mango & Fennel Salsa (see page 61)

Herbed Raita (see page 52)

1 Wrap the tortillas together in foil, and warm them in a preheated oven for 10 minutes.

2 Set the tortillas, duck breasts and roasted vegetables on the table. Put the Guacamole, salsas and Herbed Raita in separate dishes and arrange them around the tortillas, duck breasts and vegetables. Encourage each diner to wrap various combinations of smoked duck and other dishes in the tortillas.

Oven temperature
180°C/350°F/gas 4

Cooking time
10 minutes

Makes
4 servings

MEAT

RED MEAT HAS HAD SOMETHING of a bad press lately, but it is too nutritionally valuable to ignore entirely. The secret is to eat small amounts of lean meat only occasionally, and to surround and augment them with plenty of vegetables, grains and fruit. I can never over-emphasize the importance of vegetables: even when planning meat dishes, vegetables should figure prominently. In this section, meatballs and sausages, for instance, are lightened with aubergines; braised beef is bathed in a rich vegetable purée gravy; and roasted and sautéed meats share the billing with salsas, conserves, salads and relishes.

CUBAN PORK WITH A MANGO SALSA
combines flavourful marinating and fast "grill-roasting" to ensure succulent meat, bursting with juice.

A Spicy Salsa to Serve with Meat

The Mango-papaya Salsa served with Cuban Pork both enhances and contrasts with the flavour of the marinated meat. A chilli (as hot as you like) and red onion give the salsa bite, and fruits and herbs contribute a mixture of more delicate flavours.

MINT

MANGO

PAPAYA

MANGO-PAPAYA SALSA

CORIANDER

RED ONION

CHILLI

LIME JUICE

Cuban Pork with a Mango-papaya Salsa

INGREDIENTS

1 pork tenderloin, about 500g (1lb), very well trimmed

For the marinade

125ml (4fl oz) orange juice

3 tbsp lemon juice

250ml (8fl oz) water

2 tbsp lime juice

½ head garlic, cloves crushed

2 tbsp soy sauce

freshly ground black pepper

2 tbsp dried oregano

4 bay leaves

For the Mango-papaya Salsa

1 mango, diced (see page 136)

1 papaya, diced

1 small red onion, diced

3 tbsp lime juice

1 chilli, deseeded and chopped

2 tbsp chopped fresh coriander

2 tbsp shredded fresh mint

1 Put the pork in a shallow glass dish. Mix together the marinade ingredients and pour over the pork. Leave for 30 minutes–24 hours, turning the meat in the marinade occasionally.

2 Line a roasting tin with foil. Pour in water to a depth of 1cm (½in). Lightly oil-water spray a wire rack and put in the tin. Put the pork on the rack, reserving the marinade. Roast in a preheated oven for 20–25 minutes, turning it after 12 minutes and basting with marinade.

3 While the meat is cooking, mix together the salsa ingredients to serve with the pork.

4 Remove the pork from the oven and leave to rest for 5–10 minutes. To serve, slice thinly across, slightly on the diagonal.

VARIATION

Korean Pork Marinade: 1 tbsp crushed root ginger, ½ head garlic, crushed, 1 bunch spring onions, sliced, 125g (4oz) sugar, 125ml (4fl oz) Teriyaki or soy sauce, 250ml (8fl oz) water. Serve Korean Pork with an oriental dipping sauce.

Per serving	
Total fat (g)	5
Saturated fat (g)	2
Unsaturated fat (g)	3
Cholesterol (mg)	75
Sodium (mg)	171
Calories	234

Oven temperature
240°C/450°F/gas 9

Cooking time
20–25 minutes

Makes
4 servings

SPICY, CITRUS-SCENTED MEXICAN SAUSAGES

The meat for these sausages is very, very lean, and the aubergine ensures it is succulent. Go for a gorgeous presentation for these characterful delicacies, serving them on tortillas with rich sauces such as Tomato, Garlic & Pepper Sauce (see page 64) or Cherry Tomato & Red Onion Salsa (see page 61). If you prefer, replace the lean pork with turkey meat in all three recipes here.

INGREDIENTS

250g (8oz) extra-lean pork tenderloin, trimmed and minced

one 250g (8oz) aubergine, roasted, peeled and chopped (see page 37)

2 spring onions, chopped

375g (12oz), plus 3 tbsp, fresh breadcrumbs

1 tbsp chopped fresh parsley

1 tbsp chopped fresh mint

1 tbsp chopped fresh coriander

½ tsp ground cumin

½ tsp ground coriander

pinch or two of chilli powder

salt and freshly ground black pepper

juice and grated zest of ¼ large orange

juice and grated zest of ½ lime

3 egg whites, lightly beaten

8 tbsp plain flour

600ml (1 pint) stock (see page 30)

600ml (1 pint) dry red wine

4–6 red or yellow peppers, cored, deseeded, peeled and cut into strips (see page 34)

finely chopped fresh coriander, to garnish

1 Mix together thoroughly the pork, aubergine, spring onions, 3 tablespoons of breadcrumbs, herbs, spices, salt and pepper, and the citrus juices and zest (use your hands for best results). Fry a tiny piece of the mixture in a non-stick frying pan and taste for seasoning, adjusting as necessary.

2 Form the mixture into 8–10 oval-shaped sausage patties.

3 Pour the egg whites into a soup plate. Spread the flour on another plate. Sprinkle the remaining breadcrumbs on yet another plate and season lightly with salt and pepper.

4 Dredge each sausage patty on all sides in flour, then coat each one in egg white and then in the crumbs. Press firmly to ensure that the crumbs adhere during cooking. Set aside.

5 Mist a heavy non-stick frying pan lightly with oil-water spray, and heat. Put in the sausages. Cook over a moderately high heat until crusty and browned on one side, then turn carefully and cook on the second side until crusty brown. Transfer the sausages to a warm plate.

6 Pour approximately 350ml (12fl oz) each of the stock and wine into the frying pan. Boil rapidly for a few seconds, deglazing the pan by scraping up the browned bits of sausage on the bottom. Add another 175ml (6fl oz) each of stock and wine.

7 Return the sausages to the pan. Simmer over a medium heat for several minutes, turning them carefully from time to time.

8 When the sausages are beautifully glazed and the pan juices are scant, thick and syrupy, transfer the sausages and sauce to a platter and cover loosely with a tent of foil to keep warm. If you are serving the sausages with a sauce or salsa, as I suggest above, the platter could have a layer of warmed sauce on it, with the sausages arranged on top.

9 Meanwhile, pour the remaining stock and wine into a second frying pan or a wok and add the pepper strips. Stir fry until the peppers are tender and the pan juices are rich and syrupy. Serve the sausages with the pepper strips and garnished with the chopped coriander.

Per serving

Total fat (g)	6
Saturated fat (g)	2
Unsaturated fat (g)	4
Cholesterol (mg)	38
Sodium (mg)	989
Calories	670

Makes
4 servings

CRUSTY "GRILL-FRIED" PORK ESCALOPES

Pork cutlets are splendid served with a highly coloured vegetable purée sauce and pan-fried mushrooms or Sicilian Vegetable Salsa (see page 63). They also make a magnificent sandwich filling: try them sandwiched between homemade bread with a good salsa, perhaps embellished with stir-fried peppers or Sweet & Sour Red Onions (see page 70). They will make a sandwich to cherish.

INGREDIENTS

salt and freshly ground black pepper

2–3 tbsp plain flour

about 16 tbsp fresh breadcrumbs

a good pinch of paprika

2–3 tbsp grated Parmesan

8 thin boneless pork loin chops, about 5mm–1cm (¼–½in) thick, total weight 400g/13oz, trimmed of all fat

4 egg whites, lightly beaten with a few dashes of Tabasco and Worcestershire sauces and ½ tsp Balsamic vinegar

olive oil-water spray (see page 29)

lemon or lime wedges, to garnish

1 Season the flour and spread it on a plate. Mix together the breadcrumbs, paprika and Parmesan. Dredge the chops in the flour then dip into the egg white mixture, coating each chop well. Dredge the chops in the crumbs. Re-dip into the egg and then the crumbs. If possible, chill for 1–2 hours to help the coating adhere.

2 Oil-water spray a non-stick baking sheet and heat under a preheated grill. Remove carefully, respray, and put the chops, well spaced, on the sheet. Spray the chops, and grill 12cm (5in) from the heat for 3 minutes or so.

3 Turn, spray again and grill until browned, sizzling and just cooked through. Serve the escalopes on a warmed platter with lemon or lime wedges and a sauce of your choice (see introduction).

Per serving

Total fat (g)	12
Saturated fat (g)	5
Unsaturated fat (g)	7
Cholesterol (mg)	80
Sodium (mg)	704
Calories	456

Makes
4 servings

PIQUANT LEMON HERB MEATBALLS

These are delicate, fragrant and juicy little patties. It's the aubergine that imparts the delicacy and juiciness – under ordinary circumstances, meatballs from very lean mince resemble cannonballs. Serve hot or cold, on their own (with lemon and mint) or in pitta breads with salsa or relish, or on a bed of sauce, such as Tomato Aubergine Sauce (see page 62).

INGREDIENTS

500g (1lb) extra-lean pork tenderloin, trimmed and minced

3 tbsp lemon juice, plus extra to taste

grated zest of ½ lemon

1 tbsp each chopped fresh coriander, parsley and mint

1 tsp each ground cumin and ground coriander

½ tsp ground paprika

several dashes of Tabasco sauce

good pinch of chilli powder, or to taste

two 180g (6oz) aubergines, roasted, peeled and chopped (see page 36)

salt and freshly ground black pepper

1 In a large bowl, thoroughly mix together all of the ingredients. Fry a tiny piece of the mixture in a non-stick pan and taste for seasonings, adding more salt, pepper, chilli powder or lemon juice, as you want for a good, spicy flavour.

2 Form the mixture into small patties and place on a platter. Spritz a non-stick frying pan with oil-water spray, and heat. Pan-fry the patties in batches (they should be well spaced) for about 2–3 minutes on each side until they are well browned and just cooked through.

Per serving

Total fat (g)	6
Saturated fat (g)	3
Unsaturated fat (g)	3
Cholesterol (mg)	47
Sodium (mg)	461
Calories	287

Makes
6 servings

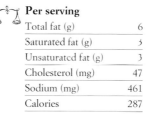

BEEF BRAISED IN RED WINE WITH A RICH GRAVY

Brisket is a remarkable cut of meat. Once the layers of fat have been trimmed away, it is a flattish, lean cut with a deep and satisfying old-fashioned beefiness: it is by far the best cut for slow braising. Here it is braised with red wine and vegetables, which are then puréed with the pan juices to form a rich, thick sauce that rivals any traditional gravy. I like plenty of watercress, or a dark green salad served alongside.

INGREDIENTS

1 boneless beef brisket, about 2kg (4lb), unrolled and trimmed of all fat

175ml (6fl oz) stock (see page 30), plus extra (see method)

3 large red onions, sliced

3 red peppers, cored, deseeded and cut into strips

250ml (8fl oz) dry red wine

175ml (6fl oz) passata

1 large carrot, sliced

8–10 garlic cloves, peeled

1 chilli, coarsely chopped (optional)

salt and freshly ground black pepper

1 Oil-water spray a large non-stick frying pan. Heat the pan, add the beef and sear on both sides. Transfer to a plate and loosely cover with foil. Pour out any fat drippings.

2 Blot the pan lightly with kitchen paper then pour in the stock and add the onions. Cover, and boil for 4–5 minutes. Uncover, reduce the heat, and cook gently.

3 When the onions are brown and almost tender, add the peppers. Stir and cook until the liquid has evaporated and the peppers are tender, adding more stock as needed. Scrape up the browned bits in the pan as you stir.

4 Meanwhile, pour the wine and passata into a pan. Boil until reduced slightly and thickened.

5 Spread the onions and peppers out in a baking dish. Add the carrot, garlic and chilli. Pour in any meat juices from the beef. Set the meat on the vegetables and season. Pour the wine-tomato mixture over and around the meat.

Per serving

Total fat (g)	21
Saturated fat (g)	9
Unsaturated fat (g)	11
Cholesterol (mg)	180
Sodium (mg)	263
Calories	556

 Oven temperature
180°C/350°F/gas 4, then 120°C/250°F/gas ½

 Oven cooking time
3–3½ hours

Makes
6 servings

6 Cover the dish with foil, making sure it does not touch the meat. Cook in a preheated oven for 1 hour. Reduce the oven temperature to the lower setting and cook for an additional 2–2½ hours, or until very tender.

7 Remove the meat to a plate and cover it. Pour the pan juices and vegetables into a jug, adding any juices that have accumulated under the meat, and cover the jug. Leave the beef to cool completely, then wrap it in clingfilm. Chill the beef, juices and vegetables in the refrigerator for up to two days. (Chilling sets the beef, making it easy to carve into slices.)

8 Skim any fat from the chilled vegetables and juices in the jug. Purée the vegetables and juices in a blender, then rub them through a sieve, to make a wonderfully smooth sauce.

9 Carve the meat thinly against the grain and arrange in a baking dish. Pour over some of the puréed vegetable sauce. Either reheat or cover with clingfilm and chill until ready to use. To reheat, cover the baking dish with foil and cook for 35–40 minutes in an oven preheated to moderate, 160°C/325°F/gas 3. Reheat any remaining sauce and serve in a warmed gravy boat.

PAN-SAUTEED BEEF STEAK IN RED WINE GARLIC SAUCE

It is essential to use good beef for this recipe. Many supermarkets are now carrying excellent quality beef, which is worth the extra expense. I would serve these steaks with Oven-fried Potatoes (see page 72) and watercress. When the ingredients are top notch, it makes a great dish.

INGREDIENTS

freshly ground black pepper

2 sirloin steaks, each about 150g (5oz), cut 5mm–1 cm (¼–½in) thick, trimmed of fat

salt

1 small red onion, quartered and thinly sliced

2–3 garlic cloves, crushed

several dashes of Tabasco sauce

300ml (½ pint) dry red wine

300ml (½ pint) stock (see page 30)

1½ tbsp Dijon mustard or red pepper Dijon mustard

1 Grind a generous amount of pepper on to a plate, place the steaks on the pepper, and grind more on top. Press the pepper into the steaks.

2 Spritz a heavy-based non-stick frying pan with oil-water spray, and heat until it sizzles. Lay the steaks, well spaced, in the pan and season with salt. Sear over a high heat for about 1 minute, turn, salt lightly and sear for

another minute. Transfer the steaks to a plate.

3 Add the onion, garlic, Tabasco and 125ml (4fl oz) each of wine and stock. Cover and boil rapidly for 2–3 minutes, then uncover and simmer briskly until the onions are tender and the juices have reduced to a syrupy sauce. Pour in the juices that have accumulated under the steaks.

4 Put the steaks in the pan and cook in the sauce, turning frequently, for 1–2 minutes, or according to taste. Return to the plate and cover loosely with foil.

5 Add the remaining wine and stock to the pan and boil until reduced by just over half and the alcohol has completely evaporated. Whisk in the mustard and simmer briskly for 2 minutes to thicken the sauce and blend the flavours. Return the steaks to the pan and turn them in the sauce until warmed through. Serve the steaks with the sauce poured over the top.

 Per serving

Total fat (g)	11
Saturated fat (g)	4
Unsaturated fat (g)	6
Cholesterol (mg)	81
Sodium (mg)	556
Calories	282

 Makes
2 servings

VENISON STEAKS WITH GRILLED PEPPER PUREE

Venison is a remarkably low-fat, flavoured meat. Even farmed venison has a hint of wild gaminess, certainly more so than beef, and it marries well with assertive, but not overwhelming, flavours. Here, it is served with a smoky grilled pepper purée and an onion conserve flavoured with a bitter orange marmalade.

INGREDIENTS

For the onion conserve

2 large red onions, halved and sliced into thin crescents

6 large garlic cloves, crushed

juice of ½ large orange

1 tbsp lemon juice

350ml (12fl oz) stock (see page 30)

175ml (6fl oz) dry red wine

1 tsp Seville orange marmalade

2 tsp French mustard

several dashes of Tabasco sauce

dash or two of Worcestershire sauce

For the pepper purée

2 red or yellow peppers, grilled (see page 35)

salt and freshly ground black pepper

For the venison steaks

black peppercorns

4 venison steaks cut 2.5–3.5 cm (1–1½in) thick, each about 125g (4oz)

1–2 tbsp dry red wine

1–2 tbsp stock (see page 30)

1 For the conserve, put the onions, garlic, citrus juices, 300ml (½ pint) of stock and 125ml (4fl oz) of wine in a heavy-based, non-stick frying pan. Cover, bring to the boil, and simmer briskly for 5–7 minutes.

2 Remove the cover and continue to cook rapidly until the liquid is almost gone and the onions are tender, but not mushy, and "frying" in their own juices.

3 Stir in the remaining stock and wine and simmer briskly for a few seconds. Stir in the marmalade, mustard and sauces. Simmer for another 1–2 minutes, until the mixture has thickened and the flavours have blended. Set the conserve aside.

4 To make the pepper purée, purée the peppers in a blender until smooth. Season with salt and pepper and heat gently. Set aside and keep warm.

5 For the venison, grind a generous amount of pepper on to a plate. Press the venison steaks on to the pepper, and grind more pepper on top of them.

6 Spritz a heavy based non-stick pan with oil-water spray, and heat until hot and sizzling. Cook the steaks over a high heat, turning them two or three times, until well-browned on the outside but still quite rare.

7 Pour the wine and stock into the pan. Continue cooking for about 5 minutes until the venison is glazed and cooked through, but still pinkish inside. The meat should feel springy (not hard or mushy). Remove to a warm plate.

SERVING THE VENISON

1 Pour the conserve into the pan in which the steaks were cooked. Bring to the boil and simmer for a few minutes, scraping up any browned bits on the bottom of the pan, until the conserve is heated through.

2 Pour the warm pepper purée on to a heated serving platter. Slice the venison steaks across the grain and arrange on the purée. Spoon the conserve over the top.

3 A green vegetable, such as baby spinach or ruby chard, or finely sliced courgettes, makes an excellent accompaniment.

Per serving

Total fat (g)	3
Saturated fat (g)	1
Unsaturated fat (g)	2
Cholesterol (mg)	63
Sodium (mg)	237
Calories	220

Makes
4 servings

FISH & SHELLFISH

FISH IS SUPERB FOOD from both a nutritional and a gastronomic point of view. Low in calories, high in protein and B vitamins, it is a dietitian's dream. The fat content of fish varies with the species, but even fatty fish is believed to be healthy. Recent scientific and medical studies suggest that the Omega-3 fatty acids in fish oils have a beneficial effect on the heart. Overcooked fish is dry and unpalatable, so cook fish just long enough to become opaque. A good rule of thumb for roasting and oven poaching is to measure the fish at its thickest point, and then to cook at high heat for 9–10 minutes per 2.5cm (1in) of thickness.

CAJUN PRAWNS

This dish was inspired by a New Orleans classic that calls for a pound of butter and a loaf of crusty bread to sop it all up. The butter is history (oh, my arteries!) but the bread is a great idea – the juices, even without the fat, are fabulous and just beg to be soaked up.

INGREDIENTS

4 garlic cloves

4 black olives (Calamata if possible), slivered off their stones

1 red chilli, deseeded and finely chopped

1 tbsp snipped fresh rosemary

1 tsp paprika

1 tsp green peppercorns in brine, plus 1 tsp of the brine

about 2 tbsp lemon juice

300ml (½ pint) chicken or vegetable stock (see page 30)

salt and freshly ground black pepper

2 dashes of Worcestershire sauce

175ml (6fl oz) fish stock (see page 30)

1kg (2lb) raw, headless king prawns, shelled and deveined

For the garnish

chopped fresh flat-leaf parsley

torn fresh oregano leaves

1 Crush the garlic and olives together into a pulp. Place in a wok with all the ingredients up to and including the Worcestershire sauce. Bring to the boil and reduce by about two-thirds.

2 Add the fish stock, bring back to the boil and reduce the liquid by half again. Tip in the prawns and stir over the highest heat for about 3 minutes, until pink and beginning to curl. Take care not to overcook them or they will turn mealy; taste one to check.

3 Sprinkle with the fresh herbs and serve at once with Flavour-infused Bulgar (see page 114) or a good dish of rice.

VARIATIONS

Cajun Mussels: replace the prawns with 1 kg (2lb) cleaned mussels (discarding any that do not close when tapped). Using a deep, heavy-based saucepan instead of the wok, follow step 1, above. Add the fish stock and bring to the boil. Tip in the mussels and cook until they open, about 4–6 minutes. Shake the pan halfway through cooking and discard any mussels that do not open. Sprinkle over the herbs.

Cajun Monkfish: slice the 2 fillets from a skinned and boned monkfish tail (see page 103) into 1cm (½in) medallions. Follow step 1, above. Add the fish stock and reduce by half. Oil-water spray a non-stick heavy-based frying pan, add the monkfish medallions and sear on both sides to seal. Pour in the reduced liquid and bring back to the boil. Sprinkle over the fresh herbs.

 Per serving

Total fat (g)	2
Saturated fat (g)	neg
Unsaturated fat (g)	1
Cholesterol (mg)	488
Sodium (mg)	762
Calories	220

 Makes
4 servings

CAJUN PRAWNS *with the hot flavour of chillies.*

MUSSELS STEAMED IN HERBED WHITE WINE

I like serving these mussels piled high on a beautiful platter, as a first course on their own, or as part of an antipasti selection. This recipe is also gorgeous with fresh small clams.

INGREDIENTS

1kg (2lb) mussels

300ml (½ pint) dry white wine or dry white vermouth

150ml (¼ pint) water

1 large onion, finely chopped

4 spring onions, trimmed and sliced

2 tbsp chopped fresh parsley

4 sprigs fresh thyme

1 double quantity aubergine infusion (see page 62: Bolognese Sauce, step 1)

1–2 tbsp breadcrumbs

grated Parmesan, to garnish (optional)

1 Scrub the mussels to remove any grit and traces of barnacles, and pull and scrape away their wispy beards. Discard any mussels that are cracked or abnormally heavy. Tap and squeeze any mussels that are not tightly closed. If they do not immediately close tight, discard them. Swish the remaining mussels around in a large bowl of cold water, drain, then rinse and drain once more.

2 Put the wine, water, onion, spring onions and herbs in a deep, heavy pan. Bring to the boil.

3 Tip in the mussels and cover the pan. Simmer for 4–6 minutes until they open. Using oven gloves, pick up the pan half-way through, and give it a good shake. Discard any mussels that do not open.

4 Roughly purée the aubergine infusion in a food processor, then stir in the breadcrumbs. When the mussels are cooked, preheat the grill. Remove the top shell from each mussel. Top the mussel meat within its shell with a spoonful of the aubergine mixture. If you like cheese with shellfish, sprinkle with a little grated Parmesan. Flash briefly under the grill to brown, then serve at once.

 Per serving

Total fat (g)	6.5
Saturated fat (g)	1.5
Unsaturated fat (g)	4.5
Cholesterol (mg)	103
Sodium (mg)	1028
Calories	375

 Makes
4 servings

TUNA MARINATED IN LEMON & GARLIC

Tuna is a substantial fish, disastrously dry when overcooked, juicy and meaty when properly cooked. It is at its best when still slightly pink in the centre. To achieve perfect results, cook it for a little less time than is usually recommended for fish cooking (see section introduction, page 100).

INGREDIENTS

2 tuna steaks, each about 1.5–2.5cm (¾–1in) thick

125–150ml (4–5fl oz) freshly squeezed lemon juice

2 tbsp dry white vermouth

2 garlic cloves, crushed

freshly ground black pepper

6 tbsp each red and yellow Pepper Sauces (see page 64)

1 Place the tuna in a baking dish. Sprinkle with 125ml (4fl oz) of lemon juice. Sprinkle on the vermouth and garlic, and season with pepper. Turn the fish in the marinade a few times. Cover with clingfilm and chill for a few hours or overnight. Turn once or twice during marinating.

2 Bring to room temperature. If most of the marinade has been absorbed into the fish, squeeze over a tablespoon of lemon juice.

3 Bake the fish, uncovered, in a preheated oven for about 8–9 minutes, until a bit rare and not at all dry. Serve at once on a bed of the red and yellow pepper sauces.

VARIATION

Substitute fresh swordfish for tuna. The same rules of rareness apply.

 Per serving

Total fat (g)	7
Saturated fat (g)	2
Unsaturated fat (g)	5
Cholesterol (mg)	42
Sodium (mg)	106
Calories	265

 Oven temperature
230°C/450°F/gas 8

 Cooking time
9 minutes

 Makes
2 servings

ROASTED MONKFISH WITH GARLIC SAUCE

Until quite recently, monkfish was often called "poor man's lobster" because of the delicate flavour of its pearly white flesh. Today, we appreciate monkfish not just for its flavour and lack of bones, but for its firm flesh, ideal for roasting or barbecuing. The ruby dark, winey sauce in this recipe sets the flesh off perfectly.

INGREDIENTS

12 garlic cloves, peeled

200ml (7fl oz) dry red wine

200ml (7fl oz) stock (see page 30)

oil-water spray (see page 29)

2 x 125g (4oz) monkfish fillets, skin and membrane removed (see below)

salt and freshly ground black pepper

2 sun-dried tomatoes, chopped

1½ tsp Dijon mustard

chopped flat-leaf parsley, to garnish

1 Put 10 of the garlic cloves in a saucepan with 125ml (4fl oz) each of wine and stock. Simmer until the garlic is meltingly tender, and coated in syrupy glaze.

2 Reduce the garlic to a purée by pushing it through a fine-meshed sieve into a bowl. Set aside. Roughly crush the 2 remaining garlic cloves and set aside.

3 Oil-water spray an ovenproof frying pan and heat it on the stove. When smoking, brown the monkfish on all sides, turning it, for a total of 1½–2 minutes. Season with salt and pepper.

4 Put the frying pan into a preheated oven and bake for 7 minutes. Do not overcook the fish, which should be juicy and pearly (not tough, dry and fibrous). When pressed, the fillets should feel firm yet springy.

5 Meanwhile, put the remaining garlic in a saucepan with the remaining stock and wine, and sun-dried tomatoes. Boil for 2–3 minutes until reduced by half, then whisk in the mustard and the puréed garlic mixture and simmer gently for another minute.

6 Transfer the monkfish to a carving board and slice into 1cm (½in) medallions. Overlap them on a warm plate, and spoon the garlic sauce around the slices. Sprinkle with parsley and serve at once. Yellow vegetables, such as yellow tomato slices or yellow pepper strips, make vivid accompaniments for this dish.

 Per serving

Total fat (g)	2
Saturated fat (g)	neg
Unsaturated fat (g)	1
Cholesterol (mg)	18
Sodium (mg)	196
Calories	156

 Oven temperature
220°C/425°F/gas 7

 Oven cooking time
7 minutes

 Makes
2 servings

PREPARING MONKFISH

1 Using kitchen scissors or a very sharp small knife, and cutting close to the flesh, snip off the two fins from the monkfish and discard them.

2 Pull off and discard the skin and tough membrane covering the monkfish, being careful not to tear the flesh.

3 Using a large chef's knife or a fish filleting knife, slice down one side of the backbone, keeping as close to the bone as possible, to remove the first fillet in one piece.

4 Cut along the other side of the backbone to remove the second fillet, again in one piece. (Do not discard the backbone, which may be used to make a fish stock.)

SALMON WITH YELLOW PEPPER & TARRAGON SAUCE

Salmon is a fatty fish, but the Omega-3 fatty acids in fish oil are believed to be very heart-healthy. This Technicolor extravaganza (coral-tinted fish, blazingly yellow sauce, pastel salsa) complements the moist, delicate fish very well indeed.

INGREDIENTS

450ml (¾ pint) yellow Pepper Sauce (see page 64 and step 1 below)

2 salmon fillets, each about 150–180g (5–6oz)

freshly ground mixed peppercorns

salt

oil-water spray (see page 29)

2 sprigs fresh tarragon

1 quantity Mango & Fennel Salsa (see page 61)

1 Prepare the yellow Pepper Sauce according to the recipe on page 64, but replace the garlic and chilli with a pinch of cayenne and a teaspoon of crumbled dried tarragon.

2 Season the salmon on both sides with a generous amount of ground mixed pepper and salt. Spray a lidded frying pan with oil-water spray and heat on the stove. Sear the salmon on both sides, flesh side first, for 1½ minutes in total, until browned.

3 Immediately cover the pan tightly, remove from the heat and leave for 3–4 minutes, until the salmon is just done. The flesh should remain sweetly moist and succulent.

4 Coat two plates with a layer of sauce, and centre a fillet on each one. Top with a sprig of fresh tarragon and surround with Mango & Fennel Salsa.

 Per serving

Total fat (g)	20
Saturated fat (g)	3
Unsaturated fat (g)	15
Cholesterol (mg)	83
Sodium (mg)	176
Calories	505

Makes
2 servings

HALIBUT ROASTED IN TOMATO AUBERGINE SAUCE

Halibut is delicious roasted on a bed of velvety Tomato Aubergine Sauce (see page 62). It is important the fish sits on the sauce: don't swamp it by pouring the sauce over the top. Cooked this way, the fillets melt in the mouth.

INGREDIENTS

375g (12oz) small new potatoes (about 16)

2 halibut fillets, each about 180–250g (6–8oz), any bones removed with tweezers

salt and freshly ground black pepper

600ml (1 pint) Tomato Aubergine Sauce (see page 62)

For the garnish

torn fresh basil leaves

fresh flat-leaf parsley, roughly chopped

1 Bring a pan of water to the boil. Meanwhile, wash the potatoes under cold running water. When the water is boiling, steam the potatoes over the water for about 15–20 minutes, until just done.

2 Season the halibut fillets with salt and pepper.

3 Pour the Tomato Aubergine Sauce into an ovenproof frying pan, casserole or baking dish that will hold the fillets in one uncrowded layer. Bring to the boil and let the sauce simmer for a few minutes.

4 Set the fillets, spaced well apart, in the bubbling sauce and arrange the potatoes all round. Immediately transfer the uncovered dish to a preheated oven. Oven-roast the dish for 9–10 minutes per 2.5cm (1in) thickness of fish (see section introduction, page 100).

5 Scatter the basil and parsley over the top and serve the halibut straight from the pan, on to well warmed plates.

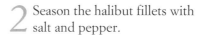 **Per serving**

Total fat (g)	6
Saturated fat (g)	1
Unsaturated fat (g)	5
Cholesterol (mg)	90
Sodium (mg)	355
Calories	378

 Oven temperature
230°C/450°F/gas 8

 Cooking time
9–10 minutes per 2.5cm (1 inch) thickness of fish

 Makes
2 servings

ROASTED BLACK BEAN COD

Marinate the cod with ginger, then roast it quickly in a hot oven so that it falls into ineffably moist, milky flakes. Set off that moist milkiness with a salty, peppery black bean sauce and encircle with a fresh tomato-based salsa.

INGREDIENTS

1 large garlic clove

1cm (½in) piece fresh ginger, peeled

2 tsp Teriyaki sauce

1 tsp rice wine vinegar

1 cod fillet, about 375g (12oz)

freshly ground black pepper

oil-water spray (see page 29)

1 quantity Black Bean Tomato Sauce (see page 66)

1 quantity Chinese Tomato Salsa (see page 67)

1 Crush together the garlic and ginger and put in a bowl with the Teriyaki sauce and vinegar.

2 Put the cod on a plate and pour over the garlic-ginger mixture. Grind over some pepper. Leave it to marinate at room temperature for approximately 20 minutes.

3 Mist a baking sheet with oil-water spray. Put the cod on the tray, scraping all the marinade over the fish. Spray with oil-water, and roast for approximately 9–10 minutes per 2.5cm (1in) thickness of fish.

4 Spoon the heated Black Bean Tomato Sauce on to a plate, set the fish on top, then surround with the Chinese Tomato Salsa.

Per serving

Total fat (g)	4
Saturated fat (g)	1
Unsaturated fat (g)	3
Cholesterol (mg)	86
Sodium (mg)	1571
Calories	304

Oven temperature
220°C/425°F/gas 7

Baking time
9–10 minutes per 2.5cm (1 inch) thickness of fish

Makes
2 servings

PASTA

PASTA IS EXEMPLARY FOOD: quick to cook, inspiring in its variety, supremely comforting and very low in fat. Traditional pasta sauces, however, are very high-fat, laden as they are with butter, olive oil and fatty cheeses. But it doesn't have to be that way: sauces based on vegetables, vegetable stock, low- and medium-fat cheeses, with lively seasoning and plenty of fresh herbs, make luscious pasta dressings, and are nutritionally savvy. I like sauces to be plentiful so I ladle them over the pasta with abandon. A serving of pasta is anything from 60–150g (2–5oz), depending on how it is to be served and the sauce accompanying it.

PASTA WITH AN ORIENTAL AIR

Dress a tangle of the thinnest pasta with an Oriental sauce studded with mushrooms, courgettes, and salty black beans, and top the whole thing with Chinese Tomato Salsa for an exuberant vegetarian dish. If you crave meat, add a few slices of pork tenderloin roasted in Korean Pork Marinade (see page 93).

INGREDIENTS

1cm (½in) piece fresh root ginger, peeled

2 garlic cloves

1 red onion, cut into chunks

300ml (½ pint) chicken or vegetable stock (see page 30)

125g (4oz) closed-cup mushrooms, quartered

60ml (2fl oz) sherry

dash or two of Teriyaki sauce

375g (12oz) courgettes, trimmed and diced

250g (8oz) vermicelli (preferably angel hair)

125ml (4fl oz) passata

2 tbsp black bean sauce

2 tbsp Hoisin sauce

2 tbsp Chinese chilli sauce

a few drops of lime juice

For the garnish

chopped fresh coriander

2 or 3 spring onions, including the green tops, sliced

1 quantity Chinese Tomato Salsa (see page 67)

1 Crush together the ginger and garlic and put into a wok with the onion and stock. Simmer briskly until reduced by half.

2 Add the mushrooms, sherry and Teriyaki. Simmer briskly for a few minutes, stirring continuously, until the mushrooms are slightly more than half-cooked. Add the courgettes, stir and cook for 2–3 minutes, until tender but still crisp.

3 Meanwhile, bring a pan of lightly salted water to the boil and cook the vermicelli until tender, about 3 minutes. Drain, cover and keep warm.

4 Whisk together the passata, black bean sauce, Hoisin and Chinese chilli sauces, and stir into the wok. Simmer for 2 minutes until bubbling and thickened, then squeeze in a few drops of lime juice to taste.

5 Toss the sauce with the warm vermicelli. Top each serving with coriander, spring onions, and a good spoonful of the Chinese Tomato Salsa.

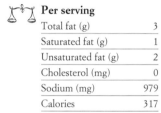

Per serving

Total fat (g)	3
Saturated fat (g)	1
Unsaturated fat (g)	2
Cholesterol (mg)	0
Sodium (mg)	979
Calories	317

Makes
4 servings

**PASTA WITH
AN ORIENTAL AIR**
*combines several Chinese
flavourings for an exotic
and unusual
pasta sauce.*

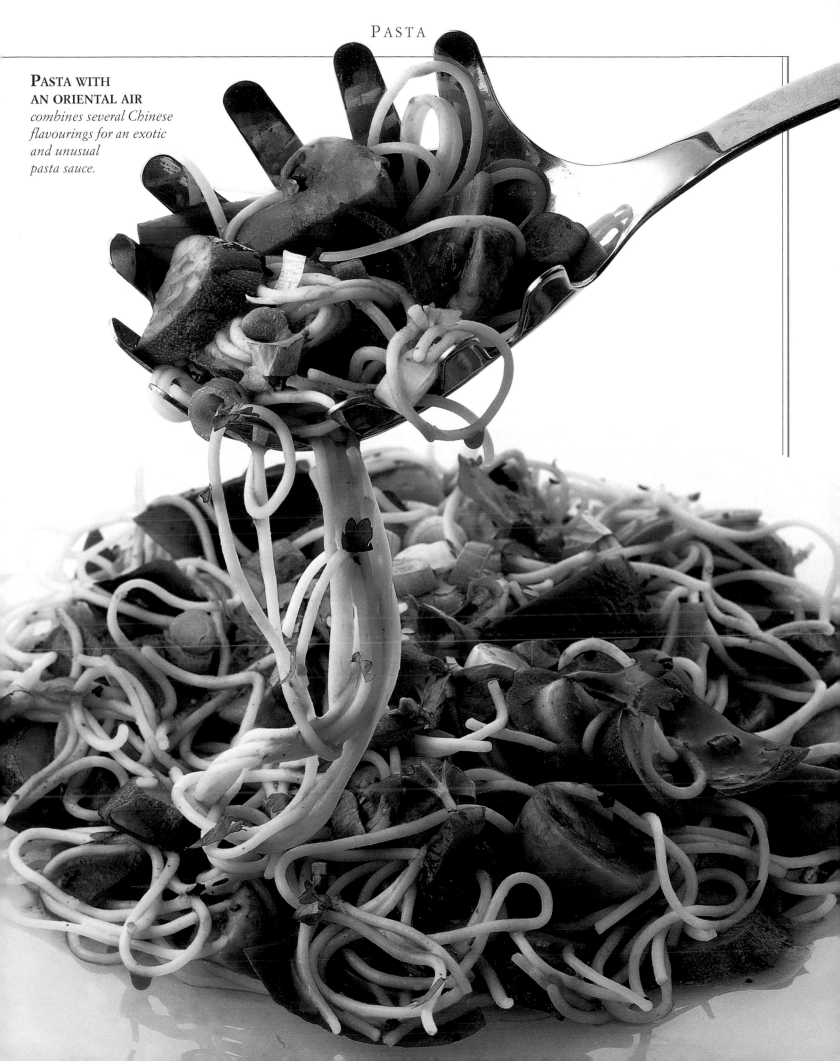

OPEN RAVIOLI WITH TWO SAUCES

This memorable first course is easy to put together if you have everything ready. Cook the asparagus and sauces ahead of time: briefly steam the asparagus (it should be hot, not overcooked) and have the sauces simmering on the hob before serving.

INGREDIENTS

4 fresh lasagne sheets

300ml (½ pint) yellow Pepper Sauce (see page 64)

8 asparagus stalks, cooked (see page 78)

300ml (½ pint) Tomato Sauce (see page 66)

freshly ground mixed pepper

1 Cook the lasagne according to package directions, or until tender. Drain and blot. Put one sheet on each of two warm plates.

2 Spoon some Pepper Sauce on the pasta, and top each one with four asparagus spears. Cover with a lasagne sheet, placing it at an angle. Pour on the Tomato Sauce, and season. Serve at once.

Per serving

Total fat (g)	4
Saturated fat (g)	1
Unsaturated fat (g)	2
Cholesterol (mg)	0
Sodium (mg)	272
Calories	358

Makes
2 servings

FARFALLE WITH MINTED PEA PUREE

A subtly flavoured, brilliant green pea purée, redolent of mint and lime, makes a highly successful sauce for this pasta shape. Strew peas, crisp asparagus tips and pieces of vivid peppers over the top for an exhilarating contrast of colours and textures.

INGREDIENTS

125g (4oz) petits pois

125g (4oz) asparagus tips

3 peppers (1 red, 1 yellow and 1 orange), skinned and deseeded (see page 35)

300ml (½ pint) stock (see page 30)

375g (12oz) farfalle

1 quantity pea purée (see Variation, page 50), thinned with a little stock

1 tbsp lime juice

torn mint leaves, to garnish

1 Steam the petit pois and asparagus tips until just done, but still bright green. Cut the peppers into 2.5cm (1in) squares and sauté in the stock, as in the recipe for Silky Stir-fried Sweet Pepper Strips (see page 71).

2 Cook the farfalle according to package instructions, until *al dente*. Warm the pea purée, stir in the lime juice, then toss with the farfalle and vegetables. Scatter with mint and serve at once.

Per serving

Total fat (g)	4
Saturated fat (g)	1
Unsaturated fat (g)	3
Cholesterol (mg)	0
Sodium (mg)	162
Calories	462

Makes
4 servings

MUSHROOM-INFUSED PASTA

A simple recipe that infuses pasta shells with the essence of wild mushrooms. This is a wonderful companion for mushroom ragoûts, pork tenderloin, and roasted chicken.

INGREDIENTS

350ml (12fl oz) vegetable or chicken stock (see page 30)

300ml (½ pint) mushroom soaking stock (see page 30)

3 spring onions, trimmed and thinly sliced

salt and freshly ground black pepper

pinch of chilli powder

dash or two of Tabasco sauce

250g (8oz) tiny pasta shells

3 tbsp each chopped flat-leaf parsley and snipped fresh chives

1 Put the stocks and spring onions into a heavy-based pan. Season with salt, pepper, chilli powder and Tabasco. Bring to the boil.

2 Add the pasta, stir and bring back to the boil. Cover tightly, reduce to the lowest heat and leave for 7 minutes, or until *al dente*. Uncover, and stir. Remove from the heat, drape a tea towel over the pan, cover and leave for 5 minutes. The pasta should be tender and most of the liquid absorbed. Stir in the herbs and serve.

Per serving

Total fat (g)	1
Saturated fat (g)	<1
Unsaturated fat (g)	<1
Cholesterol (mg)	0
Sodium (mg)	92
Calories	238

Makes
4 servings, as an accompaniment

LINGUINE WITH MUSHROOM CREAM SAUCE

Who would guess that the wickedly creamy sauce here is made with skimmed milk, skimmed milk powder and cornflour? It sounds appallingly austere, but in reality it is rich and indulgent. The dried porcini pieces and the sherry are the secret ingredients – they make the sauce memorable.

INGREDIENTS

4 garlic cloves, crushed

1 tbsp each snipped fresh rosemary and thyme leaves

4 black olives, slivered off their stones

4 sun-dried tomatoes, chopped

600ml (1 pint) stock (see page 30)

750g (1½lb) closed-cup mushrooms

15g (½oz) dried porcini, rinsed and finely snipped (see page 30)

60ml (2fl oz) dry sherry

1 tbsp Teriyaki sauce

several dashes of Tabasco sauce

3 tbsp skimmed milk powder

2 tbsp cornflour

400ml (14fl oz) skimmed milk, plus extra (see method)

500g (1lb) dried linguine

3 tbsp freshly grated Parmesan

1½ tbsp red pepper Dijon mustard

1 tbsp snipped fresh oregano leaves

salt and freshly ground black pepper

1 Put the garlic, rosemary, thyme, olives, sun-dried tomatoes and 300ml (½ pint) of stock into a wok.
Boil until the liquid is almost entirely evaporated.

2 Add the mushrooms, dried porcini, sherry and sauces. Pour in 150ml (¼ pint) of stock and cook over a high heat, stirring, for about 3 minutes, until the liquid has evaporated. Pour in the remaining stock. Cook for about 5–7 minutes, stirring, until the mushrooms are just tender and have released their juices.

3 Meanwhile, mix the milk powder and cornflour in a jug. Whisk in the skimmed milk rapidly to avoid lumps forming. Slowly stir this mixture into the sauce and cook for a minute or so, until thick and bubbling. Bring a large pan of lightly salted water to the boil. Add the linguine and cook until *al dente*.

4 Meanwhile, add the Parmesan, mustard and oregano to the sauce. Cook, stirring, for 3 minutes. If needed, stir in a little more milk to make a silky sauce. Taste, and season with salt and pepper. Drain the pasta and toss with the hot sauce.

 Per serving

Total fat (g)	9
Saturated fat (g)	4
Unsaturated fat (g)	5
Cholesterol (mg)	14
Sodium (mg)	835
Calories	655

Makes
4 servings

CONCHIGLIE WITH CHUNKY PEPPERS & HERBS

An extravagance of colourful peppers sautéed in stock to the point of silky tenderness, then tossed with basil, parsley and pasta shells or quills makes a good dish for an informal meal.

INGREDIENTS

10 mixed red or yellow peppers, peeled, deseeded and cut into 2.5cm (1in) squares (see page 34)

2 fresh chillies, deseeded and finely chopped

4 garlic cloves, coarsely chopped

350ml (12fl oz) stock (see page 30)

500g (1lb) conchiglie, penne, or other short pasta shape

15 fresh basil leaves, shredded

1 tbsp chopped fresh parsley

1 Mix together the pepper squares, chillies, garlic and stock in a heavy-based frying pan, and cook, stirring occasionally, until the peppers are tender and bathed in a syrupy sauce.

2 Cook the pasta, according to package instructions, until *al dente*, then drain and combine with the sauce.

3 Toss in the basil leaves and parsley and serve at once.

 Per serving

Total fat (g)	4
Saturated fat (g)	1
Unsaturated fat (g)	3
Cholesterol (mg)	0
Sodium (mg)	108
Calories	573

Makes
4 servings

GRILLED VEGETABLE LASAGNE

This is a simple, colourful lasagne of grilled vegetables, vivid sauce and herbs. "No-cook" lasagne sheets are better if you blanch them for 3 minutes before putting the lasagne together. The dish will then need less cooking. If liked, top the lasagne with Ricotta Parmesan Custard (see page 80) and a sprinkling of Parmesan or mozzarella before baking it (as illustrated below).

INGREDIENTS

250g (8oz) "no-cook" lasagne sheets (about 9 sheets)

salt

900ml (1½ pints) Tomato, Garlic & Pepper Sauce (see page 64)

2 aubergines, sliced and grilled (see basic recipe, page 81)

4 courgettes, sliced and grilled (see basic recipe, page 81)

about 3 tbsp each chopped fresh flat-leaf parsley and torn basil leaves

1 Blanch the lasagne sheets in rapidly boiling salted water for 3 minutes, stirring to keep the sheets separate. Refresh by running cold water into the pan until cool, then lift out and place in one layer on tea towels.

2 Spread a spoonful of the sauce in a baking dish. Top with 3 lasagne sheets. Spread some sauce over. Cut the vegetables into 1.5cm (¾in) pieces and scatter with some herbs over the sauce. Cover with 3 more sheets of lasagne. Spread on more sauce and scatter on the remaining vegetables and herbs. Top with 3 lasagne sheets, and cover with the remaining sauce.

3 Cover the dish with foil, shiny side in. The dish should be well sealed, but the foil should not touch the top of the lasagne.

4 Bake in a preheated oven for 15 minutes, then uncover and bake for 15–20 minutes until the lasagne is hot through.

5 Remove the lasagne from the oven and leave for 5 minutes, before cutting into squares to serve. Sprinkle some chopped herbs over each serving.

Per serving

Total fat (g)	2
Saturated fat (g)	<1
Unsaturated fat (g)	1
Cholesterol (mg)	0
Sodium (mg)	97
Calories	215

Oven temperature
180°C/350°F/gas 4

Baking time
30–35 minutes

Makes
6 servings

CONCHIGLIONI WITH CREAMY BROCCOLI PESTO

What a wonderful way to eat your broccoli: folded into Quark and ricotta with basil, Parmesan and a few slivers of olives, then put into large pasta shells and baked under a mantle of chunky Tomato Sauce.

INGREDIENTS

18 giant pasta shells (conchiglioni)

100g (3½oz) Quark

140g (4½oz) ricotta

180g (6oz) steamed broccoli, roughly chopped

60g (2oz) fresh flat-leaf parsley, roughly chopped

handful (about 12 leaves) basil, torn

3 black olives, slivered off their stones

4 tbsp grated Parmesan

60g (2oz) Italian-style half-fat mozzarella cheese, drained and grated

salt and freshly ground black pepper

dash or two of Tabasco sauce

1 quantity Tomato Sauce (see page 66)

1 Cook the pasta shells according to the packet directions, but undercook them slightly. Drain the pasta very well.

2 Put the Quark, ricotta, broccoli, herbs, olives, 3 tablespoons of the Parmesan, and half the mozzarella in a food processor. Season with salt, pepper and Tabasco. Process to a green-flecked cream.

3 Spoon a layer of the Tomato Sauce on to the bottom of a baking dish large enough to hold all 18 pasta shells.

4 Spoon enough of the broccoli cream into each shell to fill them. Place in the baking dish on the Tomato Sauce. When all the shells are filled and in the dish, spoon more Tomato Sauce over the filled shells. Sprinkle over the remaining Parmesan and mozzarella cheeses.

5 Cover the dish with foil so that it is well sealed, but the foil is not touching the contents.

6 Bake in a preheated oven for 15 minutes. Uncover and bake for 15–20 minutes, until the dish is bubbling and the cheese has melted on top.

Per serving

Total fat (g)	9
Saturated fat (g)	5
Unsaturated fat (g)	4
Cholesterol (mg)	25
Sodium (mg)	394
Calories	356

Oven temperature
180°C/350°F/gas 4

Baking time
30–35 minutes

Makes
6 servings

LASAGNE

Layers of pasta, Bolognese Sauce and Ricotta Parmesan Custard make a homely, comforting lasagne, perfect for family feasting.

INGREDIENTS

¼ tsp freshly grated nutmeg

1 quantity Ricotta Parmesan Custard (see page 80), uncooked

200g (7oz) "no-cook" lasagne sheets

1 quantity Bolognese Sauce (see page 62)

3–4 tbsp freshly grated Parmesan

1 Beat the nutmeg into the Ricotta Parmesan Custard. Parboil, drain and blot the lasagne sheets, as for Grilled Vegetable Lasagne (see page 110).

2 Spread a generous spoonful of Bolognese Sauce in a baking dish. Top with a layer of lasagne sheets. Spread with more sauce. Pour on a third of the custard. Top with lasagne sheets, more sauce and half the remaining custard. Finally, top with the remaining lasagne sheets, sauce and custard. Sprinkle over the Parmesan.

3 Bake, uncovered, for 30–40 minutes in a preheated oven, until the custard is set and the top is browned. To check that the custard is set, insert a thin knife into the centre of the Lasagne.

Per serving

Total fat (g)	12
Saturated fat (g)	7
Unsaturated fat (g)	5
Cholesterol (mg)	69
Sodium (mg)	385
Calories	346

Oven temperature
180°C/350°F/gas 4

Baking time
About 30–40 minutes

Makes
8 servings

GRAINS & PULSES

GRAINS AND PULSES HAVE NOURISHED POPULATIONS since ancient times. Few foods are as comforting and sustaining. Of course, in too earnest hands they can also be very worthy, stodgy and dull. But you will not find that sort of '70s wholefood ethic here. These recipes glow with warmth and comfort and are never leaden. From the vegetable-laced squares of grilled polenta below, alive with the colours and flavours of an imaginative flavour infusion, to the splendid bean stews and lentil and rice dishes later in the section, these dishes are sure to be received with acclaim.

FLAVOUR-INFUSED GRILLED POLENTA

I adore polenta, and this is the best polenta I've ever had. It's an extravaganza of colour and has an unforgettable flavour because of the flavour infusion – red onions, garlic, wine, sun-dried tomatoes, olives, with spring onions and herbs – into which the polenta is stirred.

INGREDIENTS

1.8 litres (3 pints) stock (see page 30)

125ml (4fl oz) dry red wine

2 red onions, chopped

2 garlic cloves, crushed

4 sun-dried tomatoes, chopped

4 black olives, slivered off their stones

1 chilli, deseeded and finely chopped

6 spring onions, trimmed, cut in half lengthways, then finely sliced across

salt and freshly ground black pepper

375g (12oz) quick-cooking polenta

2–3 tbsp chopped fresh parsley

oil-water spray (see page 29)

1 Put 300ml (½ pint) of the stock and all the wine into a deep, heavy-based saucepan and add the onions, garlic, sun-dried tomatoes, olives, and chilli. Cover, bring to the boil, and simmer briskly for 5–7 minutes. Uncover and continue to simmer until the onions are tender, and the liquid has greatly reduced.

2 Stir in the spring onions, and continue to simmer briskly until the liquid is almost gone.

3 Add the remaining stock, season with salt and pepper and bring to just below the boil.

4 Wearing an oven glove on your stirring hand because the mixture will bubble volcanically, pour in the polenta in a steady stream, whisking with a wire whisk as you do so. When it gets thick, change to a long-handled wooden spoon. Cook for about 5 minutes, still stirring, until smooth and cooked. Stir in the parsley, and taste for seasoning. It should be lively: bland polenta is dire.

5 Spread the mixture on to a baking sheet. There may be a small bowlful left over. Save it for a separate meal, unless you want to eat it on the spot. Cover the polenta well and chill in the refrigerator until required.

SERVING THE POLENTA

1 Cut the polenta into squares about 7 x 7cm (3 x 3in). Spray lightly with oil-water spray and grill until lightly browned.

2 Serve the grilled polenta squares hot with a selection of vegetable toppings. Particularly good are Mushrooms Made Wild (see page 74), Glazed Fennel and Sweet & Sour Red Onions (see page 70), all of which are illustrated here, and Silky Stir-fried Sweet Pepper Strips (see page 71) and Bolognese Sauce (see page 62).

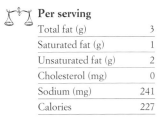

Per serving

Total fat (g)	3
Saturated fat (g)	1
Unsaturated fat (g)	2
Cholesterol (mg)	0
Sodium (mg)	241
Calories	227

Makes
8 servings

GLAZED FENNEL
(BELOW)

MUSHROOMS
MADE WILD
(RIGHT)

SWEET & SOUR
RED ONIONS
(RIGHT)

FLAVOUR-INFUSED BULGAR

A wonderful alternative to rice, bulgar has a nutty taste and tender texture, and soaks up flavour like nobody's business. Red wine gives this dish a mauve/burgundy tint.

INGREDIENTS

600ml (1 pint) stock (see page 30)

1 red onion, chopped

2 garlic cloves, crushed

4 sun-dried tomatoes, chopped

½–1 chilli, deseeded and finely chopped

4 black olives, slivered off their stones

salt and freshly ground black pepper

180g (6oz) bulgar

1 tbsp lemon juice, or to taste

For the garnish

vine tomatoes or cherry tomatoes, halved or quartered

chopped fresh flat-leaf parsley

1 Put 250ml (8fl oz) of the stock, the onion, garlic, sun-dried tomatoes, chilli and olives in a frying pan or wok. Bring to the boil, then cover and simmer briskly for 5 minutes. Uncover, and continue to simmer until the onion is tender, and "frying" in its own juices.

2 Add the remaining stock, and bring to the boil. Season with salt and pepper.

3 Put the bulgar in a heatproof bowl and pour in the boiling mixture. Cover and leave for 30 minutes, until the bulgar is tender and the liquid absorbed.

4 Uncover and squeeze in lemon juice to taste. Taste and add more salt and pepper if necessary. Drape a tea towel over the bowl and leave for 5 minutes.

5 To serve, mound on a platter, surround with the tomatoes, and sprinkle with parsley. Cajun Prawns (see page 100) go well with this, as do braised chicken, duck, venison or roast pork.

 Per serving

Total fat (g)	2
Saturated fat (g)	1
Unsaturated fat (g)	1
Cholesterol (mg)	0
Sodium (mg)	211
Calories	210

 Makes
4 servings

SPICY BORLOTTI BEANS

A generous helping of zesty beans makes a marvellous meal in a bowl with crusty bread, or wrapped in a tortilla with pea purée (see page 50) and a selection of salsas. The variation makes a no-fat "refried" bean-style dip.

INGREDIENTS

2 red onions, chopped

4 garlic cloves, crushed

3 sun-dried tomatoes, chopped

1 chilli, deseeded and chopped

1 tbsp ground cumin

½ tbsp ground coriander

375ml (13fl oz) stock (see page 30)

950g (1lb 15oz) canned borlotti beans, drained and rinsed

300ml (½ pint) passata

juice of 1 lime, plus extra to taste

2 tbsp each chopped fresh parsley, mint and coriander

salt and freshly ground black pepper

1 Mix together the onions, garlic, sun-dried tomatoes, chilli, spices and 300ml (½ pint) of stock in a frying pan. Cover and boil for 5–7 minutes. Uncover and simmer briskly until the onions are tender and the liquid is almost gone.

2 Stir in the remaining stock, the beans and passata. Simmer, partially covered, for 10 minutes, or until thick and savoury. Stir in the lime juice and herbs. Taste, and season with salt and pepper.

VARIATION

Bean dip: cool the mixture. Process to a smooth purée, adding extra lime juice. Work in more stock if needed for a soft, creamy texture.

 Per serving

Total fat (g)	2
Saturated fat (g)	1
Unsaturated fat (g)	1
Cholesterol (mg)	0
Sodium (mg)	1099
Calories	133

 Makes
4 servings

ORANGE-THYME SCENTED WILD RICE

Try serving this wild rice dish with duck and game recipes. The dried berry fruits and the orange juice complement the richer flavours of the meats wonderfully well.

INGREDIENTS

1 large red onion, chopped

pinch of dried chilli flakes

825ml (1 pint 8fl oz) stock (see page 30)

juice of ½ orange

2 tbsp dried sour cherries

2 tbsp dried cranberries

250g (8oz) wild rice

2 tsp fresh thyme leaves

salt and freshly ground black pepper

1 Put the chopped onion, the chilli flakes, 300ml (½ pint) of the stock, and the orange juice in a flameproof casserole. Simmer until the onion is tender and the liquid has almost gone. Add the dried cherries and cranberries, rice and thyme. Stir until well mixed.

2 Pour in the remaining stock and season with salt and pepper. Bring to the boil and cover the casserole tightly.

3 Bake in a preheated oven for 45–55 minutes until the rice is tender (some of the grains will puff open) and the liquid has been absorbed.

4 Drape a tea towel over the dish, replace the lid over the tea towel, and leave for a few minutes. Fluff up the rice with a fork before serving.

Per serving

Total fat (g)	1
Saturated fat (g)	neg
Unsaturated fat (g)	1
Cholesterol (mg)	0
Sodium (mg)	189
Calories	314

Oven temperature
180°C/350°F/gas 4

Baking time
45–55 minutes

Makes
4 servings

PUY LENTILS WITH WILD MUSHROOMS & HERBS

I like Puy lentils for their colour, a gorgeous deep green, flecked with turquoise, and their flavour. Both are the result of being grown in volcanic soil, round Le Puy in France. A small lentil, they do not need soaking before use.

INGREDIENTS

750ml (1¼ pints) mushroom soaking liquid (see page 30)

750ml (1¼ pints) stock (see page 30), plus extra (see method)

125ml (4fl oz) red wine

2 red onions, chopped

3 garlic cloves, crushed

275g (9oz) Puy lentils, rinsed and picked over

15g (½oz) soaked porcini, finely chopped (see page 30)

salt and freshly ground black pepper

dash of Tabasco sauce, optional

2 tbsp each chopped fresh oregano and parsley

2 tsp fresh thyme leaves

juice of ½ lemon

1 Put 150ml (¼ pint) of the mushroom soaking liquid, 150ml (¼ pint) of the stock, and all the red wine in a saucepan with the onions and garlic and bring to the boil. Cover and simmer briskly for 5 minutes.

2 Remove the cover and continue to simmer until the onions are tender, and "frying" in their syrupy juices.

3 Stir in the lentils, porcini, and the remaining mushroom soaking liquid and stock. Season generously with pepper, bring to the boil, and continue to cook, uncovered, for 10 minutes.

4 Reduce the heat and simmer, partially covered, for 30–35 minutes, stirring occasionally, until the lentils are tender. Add a little more stock if needed to prevent scorching.

5 Season well with salt, and add Tabasco sauce for an extra bite, if you like. Stir in the fresh herbs and the lemon juice.

Per serving

Total fat (g)	2
Saturated fat (g)	neg
Unsaturated fat (g)	2
Cholesterol (mg)	0
Sodium (mg)	188
Calories	281

Makes
4 servings

BORLOTTI BEAN & PARMA HAM STEW

I would describe these as a sort of heavenly baked beans (they really are marvellous). They are perfectly delicious served ladled on to slices of toasted Wild Mushroom Bread (see page 146), as illustrated below.

INGREDIENTS

olive oil-water spray (see page 29)

90g (3oz) prosciutto, trimmed of fat and diced

1 red onion, chopped

3 garlic cloves, crushed

pinch of dried chilli flakes

4 sun-dried tomatoes, chopped

½ tsp ground paprika

150ml (¼ pint) dry red wine

250ml (8fl oz) stock (see page 30)

1 red pepper, grilled, skinned, and diced (see page 35)

250ml (8fl oz) passata

1 tbsp Dijon mustard

1 tsp tomato purée

1 tbsp lemon juice

950g (1lb 15oz) canned borlotti beans, drained and rinsed

salt and freshly ground black pepper

1 Spritz a frying pan with the oil-water spray. Scatter in the prosciutto pieces and heat. When they start to sizzle, stir-fry for 1 minute. Transfer to a small bowl.

2 Add the onion to the pan with the garlic, chilli flakes, sun-dried tomatoes and paprika. Pour in the wine and stock, bring the mixture to the boil and deglaze the pan by scraping up any browned bits on the bottom of the pan.

3 Cover and simmer briskly for 5 minutes. Uncover and simmer until the liquid has gone, and the onion is "frying" in its own juices.

4 Meanwhile, put the pepper, passata, mustard, tomato purée and lemon juice in a blender and process to a purée.

5 Stir the beans into the onion mixture, then add the purée and salt and pepper. Simmer gently, partially covered, for 5–7 minutes, or until thickened.

SERVING THE BEANS

Serve the beans on slices of Wild Mushroom Bread (see page 146). Alternatively, heap them on to grilled polenta squares (see page 112), or spicy Sweet Potato Pancakes (see page 73).

Per serving

Total fat (g)	8
Saturated fat (g)	4
Unsaturated fat (g)	4
Cholesterol (mg)	0
Sodium (mg)	1775
Calories	202

Makes
4 servings

RAGOUT OF ROOTS, FENNEL & CANNELLINI BEANS

Roots are in vogue right now – I'm glad that chefs are beginning to notice that non-Mediterranean cuisines have something to offer the gastronomic world. The delicious flavours of root vegetables are enhanced by the other ingredients in this dish, and the garlic becomes quite gentle and mellow cooked this way.

INGREDIENTS

For the ragoût

1 head garlic

1 Spanish onion, halved then cut into 1cm (½in) wedges

1 fennel bulb, trimmed and cut into 1cm (½in) wedges

1 small swede, peeled and cut into 1cm (½in) pieces

1 large parsnip, peeled and cut into 1cm (½in) pieces

2 carrots, scrubbed and cut into 1cm (½in) slices

2 celery stalks, trimmed and sliced into 1cm (½in) pieces

1.25 litres (2 pints) stock (see page 30)

½ tsp dried tarragon, crumbled

1 tbsp Dijon mustard

2 tbsp tomato purée

3–4 dashes of soy sauce

125ml (4fl oz) dry red wine

3 tbsp lemon juice

salt and freshly ground black pepper

425g (14oz) canned cannellini beans, drained and rinsed

For the garnish

1 quantity White Bean, Orange & Tarragon Purée (see page 67)

fresh tarragon, snipped

1 Separate the head of garlic into individual cloves. Using a wooden mallet, hit them smartly to loosen the skin (see page 35). Remove the skins, but leave the cloves whole.

2 Put the garlic in a large pan with the other vegetables and 125ml (4fl oz) of the stock. Cover, bring to the boil and simmer for approximately 5 minutes. Remove the cover and simmer for another 5 minutes, stirring occasionally.

3 Pour in the remaining stock. Stir all the remaining ingredients except the beans into the ragoût, and season to taste. Simmer, partially covered, for 40 minutes.

4 Stir in the beans. Taste, and adjust the seasoning if necessary. Simmer for a further 10–15 minutes, until the ingredients are very tender.

5 Serve in bowls, garnishing each helping with a dollop of the White Bean, Orange & Tarragon Purée and a sprinkling of fresh tarragon.

VARIATION

For a dish with a quite different but equally delicious flavour, replace the swede and parsnip with pumpkin and acorn squash. Replace the tarragon with fresh sage leaves, snipped.

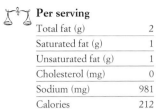

Per serving

Total fat (g)	2
Saturated fat (g)	1
Unsaturated fat (g)	1
Cholesterol (mg)	0
Sodium (mg)	981
Calories	212

Makes
6 servings

CHOCOLATE DESSERTS

LIFE WITHOUT CHOCOLATE is simply too bleak to contemplate. Fortunately, low-fat cocoa powder is pure, deep chocolate and can be used in all sorts of clever ways to produce real chocolate sensuality. Try the Chocolate Roulade, illustrated in this section, or the deceptively simple Chocolate Sorbet, for instance.

In many cases, I use a small amount of high-cocoa-solids plain chocolate to round out the flavour of a chocolate recipe. Always choose chocolate that contains at least 70 per cent cocoa solids: the higher the cocoa solids content, the lower the amount of cocoa butter. Avoid chocolate made with vegetable fat.

— CHOCOLATE ROULADE —

This mouth-watering, unbelievably rich-looking roulade is one of my star turns – no one believes it is low-fat. The base is a yolk-free soufflé baked flat. Pull out all the stops when decorating the roulade for a special occasion, as in the photograph. For more everyday meals, I give a simpler serving idea.

INGREDIENTS

For the roulade

180g (5oz) caster sugar

60g (2oz) low-fat cocoa powder (see page 43)

9 egg whites, at room temperature

pinch of cream of tartar

1½ tsp vanilla extract

1½ tsp dark rum

sifted icing sugar, for sprinkling

For the filling

1 quantity Chestnut Chocolate Cream (see page 120)

small pieces of grated chocolate (see page 43), to decorate

1 Line a 32.5 x 28cm (13 x 11in) Swiss roll tin or baking tray with non-stick baking parchment.

2 For the roulade, sift together 7 tablespoons of caster sugar with the cocoa powder. Set aside.

3 Whisk the egg whites and the cream of tartar together until foamy. Continuing to whisk briskly, add the remaining caster sugar, a little at a time, until the mixture holds stiff peaks.

4 Carefully fold the cocoa mixture into the egg whites. Fold in the vanilla and dark rum.

5 Spread the mixture into the prepared tin. Bake in a preheated oven for 20–30 minutes, or until a toothpick inserted in the middle comes out clean. Cool in the tin on a wire rack.

6 Spread a clean tea towel on the work surface. Cover with a sheet of waxed or greaseproof paper, then sprinkle evenly with icing sugar. When thoroughly cooled, turn the roulade base out on to the paper, then peel off the silicone paper.

7 Spread with the Chestnut Chocolate Cream, reserving 3–4 tablespoons, if liked, for decoration. Starting from a long edge, roll up the roulade base like a Swiss roll. Use the tea towel to help you. Cover with clingfilm and chill until needed.

8 To decorate the roulade, put the reserved filling in a nylon piping bag fitted with a medium nozzle. Pipe rosettes or a shell pattern along the top. Decorate with a few chocolate pieces, and dust with icing sugar, if liked.

VARIATION

Ice the roulade with Chocolate Icing (see page 121) and serve with Raspberry Coulis (see page 124).

Per serving

Total fat (g)	2
Saturated fat (g)	1
Unsaturated fat (g)	1
Cholesterol (mg)	neg
Sodium (mg)	189
Calories	176

Oven temperature
180°C/350°F/gas 4

Baking time
20–30 minutes

Makes
8 servings

CHOCOLATE ROULADE:
*a delightful finish for a
special occasion.*

CHESTNUT CHOCOLATE CREAM

This stand-in for high-fat buttercream makes a delicious filling for the Chocolate Roulade (see pages 118–119), or use it to sandwich Vanilla Meringue Biscuits (see page 149).

INGREDIENTS

15g (½oz) plain chocolate (see page 43)

3 tbsp icing sugar

1 tbsp low-fat cocoa powder (see page 43)

125g (4oz) chestnut purée

100g (3½oz) no-fat or very low-fat fromage frais

1 tsp vanilla extract

1 Melt the plain chocolate in a heatproof bowl over a pan of boiling water and leave to cool slightly. Sift together the icing sugar and the cocoa powder.

2 Put all of the remaining ingredients into a food processor or blender, then sprinkle in the cocoa mixture. Add the melted chocolate and process until very well combined.

3 Transfer the mixture to a bowl, then cover with clingfilm and store in the refrigerator until ready to use.

 Per recipe quantity

Total fat (g)	9
Saturated fat (g)	4
Unsaturated fat (g)	5
Cholesterol (mg)	2
Sodium (mg)	143
Calories	547

 Makes
About 300ml (½ pint)

CHOCOLATE & RASPBERRY TORTE

Raspberries and chocolate make a magnificent combination and this torte makes the most of them. It looks splendid, and the fudgy quality of the chocolate base is compelling. The torte is best eaten on the day after it is made.

INGREDIENTS

165g (5½oz) self-raising flour

180g (6oz) caster sugar

30g (1oz) low-fat cocoa powder (see page 43)

pinch salt

180g (6oz) very low-fat fromage frais

50ml (2fl oz) skimmed milk

1 tsp vanilla extract

125ml (4fl oz) water

625g (1¼lb) fresh raspberries

2 tbsp sugar

slivered zest of ½ orange and ½ lemon

For the decoration

a few raspberries and leaves

small pieces of grated plain chocolate (see page 43)

1 Sift together the flour, sugar, cocoa and salt into a bowl.

2 In a jug, mix together the fromage frais, milk, vanilla and water and pour over the dry ingredients in the bowl. Gently stir together so that the dry ingredients are thoroughly incorporated.

3 Spread the batter evenly into a 23cm (9in) springform tin. Mix together the raspberries (reserve a few for decoration), sugar and citrus zest. Pour in one even layer over the batter, leaving a 1cm (½in) border all round.

4 Bake in a preheated oven for about 30–35 minutes, then leave to cool. The raspberry centre will be wet, but will firm up as the torte cools. Cover with clingfilm and chill. Before serving, top with raspberries, raspberry leaves and a little grated chocolate.

 Per serving

Total fat (g)	1
Saturated fat (g)	<1
Unsaturated fat (g)	<1
Cholesterol (mg)	neg
Sodium (mg)	171
Calories	214

 Oven temperature
180°C/350°F/gas 4

 Baking time
30–35 minutes

Makes
8 servings

CHOCOLATE CREPES

These are lovely, delicate crêpes made with virtually no fat at all, just a spritz of oil-water spray. Fill them with orange segments, strawberries or raspberries, and a ricotta cream (see page 137). Alternatively, fill the crêpes with apricot conserve, then top with crushed Amaretti biscuits.

INGREDIENTS

90g (3oz) plain flour

2 tbsp low-fat cocoa powder (see page 43)

4 tbsp caster sugar

60g (2oz) skimmed milk powder

175ml (6fl oz) skimmed milk

4 egg whites

2 tsp vanilla extract

oil-water spray (see page 29)

1 Sift the flour, cocoa, sugar and milk powder into a bowl. Blend the milk, egg whites and vanilla in a blender until smooth. Whisk this liquid into the cocoa mixture and leave for 30 minutes.

2 Oil-water spray a frying pan and heat it on the stove. When it sizzles, carefully spray the pan again; reduce the heat to medium.

3 Using a ladle that holds about 60ml (2¼fl oz), spoon one ladleful of batter into the hot pan. Immediately tilt and rotate the pan so that the batter covers the bottom in a thin layer. Cook over high heat for a few seconds until the batter bubbles a little. Have ready a sheet of greaseproof paper.

4 Flip the crêpe over. Cook the other side for a few seconds, until the crêpe is just set, slides easily round the pan and is lightly speckled. Slide the crêpe on to the greaseproof paper. Repeat until all the batter is used.

VARIATION

Citrus-scented Vanilla Crêpes: replace the cocoa powder with an extra 30g (1oz) plain flour, and add the grated zest of 1 lemon and 1 orange.

 Per crêpe

Total fat (g)	neg
Saturated fat (g)	neg
Unsaturated fat (g)	neg
Cholesterol (mg)	1
Sodium (mg)	62
Calories	63

Makes
About 15 crêpes

DARK CHOCOLATE ICING

This wonderfully rich all-purpose icing can be used with other recipes in this book, such as the Mocha variation on the Cassata (see page 143). The recipe makes more than you will need to ice the roulades, so try serving the rest on its own as a splendidly rich and creamy old-fashioned chocolate pudding.

INGREDIENTS

9 tbsp low-fat cocoa powder (see page 43)

3 tbsp cornflour

5 tbsp skimmed milk powder

8 tbsp caster sugar

15g (½oz) plain chocolate (see page 43), grated

½ tsp vanilla extract

about 575ml (18fl oz) skimmed milk (1 long life carton)

1 Whisk together all the ingredients. Pour the mixture in batches into a liquidizer and blend until very smooth.

2 Rinse a non-stick saucepan with cold water. Pour out the water, but do not dry the pan.

3 Pour the mixture into the pan and cook on medium heat, stirring continuously, until it begins to bubble strenuously. Do not scrape the bottom of the pan: if any scorching occurs, the scorched bits will not be stirred into the mixture.

4 Still stirring, cook the mixture for another minute. Pour into a bowl immediately, cover with clingfilm and store in the refrigerator until needed.

VARIATION

Mocha Icing: add 2 tablespoons of caster sugar, and replace 175ml (6fl oz) of the skimmed milk with the same quantity of cooled black coffee.

 Per recipe quantity

Total fat (g)	15
Saturated fat (g)	9
Unsaturated fat (g)	6
Cholesterol (mg)	22
Sodium (mg)	1595
Calories	1295

 Makes
1.25 litres (2 pints)

CHOCOLATE CHEESECAKE MOUSSE

Pile this seductive mixture into a goblet, pop on an Almond Biscuit like a mini cheesecake crust, and you have a chocolate cheesecake with a difference.

INGREDIENTS

45g (1½oz) low-fat cocoa powder
(see page 43)

105g (3½oz) caster sugar

8 tbsp skimmed milk powder

125ml (4fl oz) cold water

1 tsp vanilla extract

15g (½oz) plain chocolate
(see page 43), grated

550g (1lb 2oz) ricotta

200g (7oz) Quark

1 Sift the cocoa powder, sugar and milk powder together. Put in a blender with the water and vanilla extract and blend until very smooth.

2 Rinse a heavy-based non-stick saucepan with cold water. Pour out the water, but do not dry the saucepan (this helps to reduce scorching). Strain the mixture into the pan and stir in the grated chocolate.

3 Heat on medium heat, stirring constantly, until it begins to bubble rapidly. When stirring, do not scrape the bottom of the saucepan: if any scorching does occur, this will ensure that any scorched bits are not stirred into the pudding. Continue cooking and stirring for 1 minute.

4 Remove from the heat, and pour immediately into a bowl. Cover with clingfilm and chill until needed. The sauce will become very thick and fudgy when cooled.

5 Put the cooled sauce and the ricotta and Quark into a blender and process until very smooth and fluffy. Serve the mousse in goblets, perhaps with two Almond Biscuit halves (see page 148) or two Vanilla Meringue Biscuits (see page 149) jutting out at a jaunty angle.

VARIATION

Drain the completed mousse overnight in a sieve lined with butter muslin, then swirl it into a meringue case (see page 135). Top with raspberries and a little grated plain chocolate.

 Per serving

Total fat (g)	12
Saturated fat (g)	7
Unsaturated fat (g)	4
Cholesterol (mg)	47
Sodium (mg)	219
Calories	277

 Makes
6 servings

CHOCOLATE DIPPED FRUITS

Elegant sweetmeats to serve with coffee. The chocolate dries to a brittle shell against the tender, tart-sweet fruit. The effect is deliciously sensual.

INGREDIENTS

180g (6oz) plain chocolate
(see page 43)

90g (3oz) fresh strawberries

90g (3oz) ready-to-eat dried apricots

90g (3oz) fresh cherries,
sweet if possible

90g (3oz) ready-to-eat dried
pear halves

1 Melt the chocolate gently in a heatproof bowl over a pan of hot water. Dip the strawberries, apricots and cherries in the melted chocolate, so that they are coated on one half only. Leave to cool on waxed or greaseproof paper.

2 Cut the pear halves in half lengthways. Dip the long inside edge of each piece in melted chocolate and leave to cool on the paper.

3 Put the fruits in individual pleated paper cases. Store in an airtight container in the refrigerator until ready to use.

 Per serving

Total fat (g)	9
Saturated fat (g)	5
Unsaturated fat (g)	4
Cholesterol (mg)	3
Sodium (mg)	9
Calories	222

Makes
6 servings

WICKEDLY DECADENT DEEP CHOCOLATE TRUFFLES

These are a much lower-in-fat version of a frighteningly high-fat classic. The secret ingredient is fromage frais, mixed with the very best high-cocoa-solid melted chocolate.

INGREDIENTS

180g (6oz) plain chocolate (see page 43)

180g (6oz) very low-fat fromage frais

about 2 tbsp icing sugar

½ tsp vanilla extract

15g (½oz) plain chocolate (see page 43), grated

1 Break the chocolate into a bowl over a pan of simmering water. Let it melt, stirring occasionally.

2 In a separate bowl, whisk together the fromage frais and icing sugar. Whisk in the vanilla.

3 When the chocolate is melted and smooth, remove from the heat and allow to cool slightly. Slowly whisk the chocolate into the fromage frais mixture, using a rubber scraper to incorporate every bit of chocolate. Cover with clingfilm and chill for an hour.

4 Line a baking tray with greaseproof paper. Scatter the grated chocolate on to a plate. Scoop out the chilled chocolate mixture in teaspoonfuls, roll into balls, then roll the balls in the grated chocolate and put on the prepared baking tray. Cover with clingfilm and refrigerate until firm.

5 Put the truffles in individual pleated paper cases. Store in an airtight container in the refrigerator until ready to use.

Per truffle

Total fat (g)	2
Saturated fat (g)	1
Unsaturated fat (g)	1
Cholesterol (mg)	1
Sodium (mg)	3
Calories	52

Makes
24 truffles

FRUIT DESSERTS

FRUIT SALAD MAKES A STUNNING FINISH for a meal. It is a great blessing that it does so with such high nutritional value and such low fat content. The secret is to use the best fruit, at the perfect point of fragrant ripeness. Single fruit salads, like Cherries in Cointreau, Strawberries in Balsamic Vinegar, and peaches or nectarines with Crème de Pêche, orange juice and vanilla, are dramatic, pure and intense. Fruit can also be used in many other ways, and is especially good with skimmed milk and low-fat dairy products. These ingredients may sound unadventurous, but in the guises they take on here, they are anything but.

MANGO COEUR A LA CREME

Romantic, colourful and blissfully creamy, this heart-shaped dessert would be wonderful served with a few Almond Biscuits for contrast (see page 148). It can also be made dome-shaped by draining it in a lined sieve – less romantic, but still colourful and creamy.

INGREDIENTS

For the coeur à la crème

1 large mango, cubed (see page 136)

400g (13oz) ricotta

125g (4oz) Quark

½–1 tbsp orange marmalade

few drops each orange and lemon juice

For the Mango Coulis

2 mangoes, about 300g (10oz), cubed (see page 136)

icing sugar, to taste

few drops lemon juice (optional)

1 Line a large (600ml/1 pint) coeur à la crème mould with a piece of damp butter muslin. Put the mould in a shallow pie dish or a deep plate.

2 Put the mango, ricotta and Quark in a food processor and process until smooth. Taste the mixture, and add marmalade and the citrus juices to taste, though the dominant flavour should still be mango. Process the mixture well.

3 Pile the mixture into the mould, and flip over the edges of the cloth to cover. Leave the mould, on the pie dish or plate, in the refrigerator to drain overnight.

4 For the Mango Coulis, purée the cubed mango in a food processor or blender. Sweeten to taste with the sugar, adding lemon juice if you wish to sharpen the taste a little.

5 To serve the coeur à la crème, unmould it on to a pretty plate. Surround with the Mango Coulis and serve with Tropical Fruit Salad (see page 136) or Strawberries in Lemon Balsamic Syrup (see page 128), if liked.

VARIATION

Serve the coeur à la crème with a raspberry coulis instead of the Mango Coulis. For a raspberry coulis, use two 375g (12oz) packets of frozen raspberries, thawed. Purée the fruit, then sieve it to eliminate the pips. Add icing sugar and lemon juice to taste, as for the Mango Coulis.

Per serving	
Total fat (g)	6
Saturated fat (g)	4
Unsaturated fat (g)	2
Cholesterol (mg)	25
Sodium (mg)	59
Calories	132

Makes
1 large (600ml/1 pint) coeur à la crème, or 8 individual ones

MANGO COEUR A LA CREME: *romance comes heart-shaped.*

RED VERMOUTH-BATHED SUMMER PUDDING

Both this Summer Pudding and the Winter Pudding (opposite) are splendidly healthy recipes – I love the idea of a bread-encased dome of packed fruits, the juices from the pressed fruits imbuing the bread with flavour and colour. The wines in the puddings are simmered, so the alcohol evaporates, leaving flavour, but no alcohol calories.

INGREDIENTS

1kg (2lb) frozen summer fruits, thawed

450ml (¾ pint) red vermouth

juice and zest of 1 large orange

4 tbsp lemon juice

zest of 1 large lemon

2.5cm (1in) piece cinnamon stick

1 vanilla pod

2 tbsp sugar

7–8 thin slices white bread, 1–2 days old, crusts trimmed off

1 Put the thawed fruit in a colander over a bowl and press it down to extract even more juice. Set aside and reserve all juices.

2 Put the vermouth, citrus juices and zests, cinnamon and vanilla pod in a saucepan and boil until reduced by a third. Stir in the sugar and reserved juice. Continue to boil, stirring, for 2–3 minutes. Remove from the heat, stir in the fruit and leave to cool. Remove the cinnamon and vanilla pod.

3 Cut the bread diagonally into quarters. Use most of it to line the bottom and sides of a 900ml (1½ pint) pudding basin.

4 Put the fruit mixture into the bread-lined basin. Cover the fruit with the remaining bread. Put a plate that fits in the basin on top of the pudding; place a large can on the plate to weight it. Put the pudding on a tray or plate to catch the overflow, then chill for at least 8 hours. Loosen the sides of the pudding and turn out on to a plate.

 Per serving

Total fat (g)	1
Saturated fat (g)	neg
Unsaturated fat (g)	1
Cholesterol (mg)	0
Sodium (mg)	140
Calories	135

 Makes
6 servings

SHERRY-SCENTED WINTER PUDDING

This wintertime version of Summer Pudding tastes gorgeous made with a mixture of dried fruits such as apricots, apples, sour cherries, cranberries, figs, prunes, peaches and pears.

INGREDIENTS

4 tbsp sultanas

500g (1lb) mixed dried fruit, chopped into mincemeat-size pieces

grated rind and juice of 1 lemon

350ml (12fl oz) fresh orange juice

150ml (¼ pint) cream sherry

2.5cm (1in) piece cinnamon stick

1 tsp vanilla extract

4 tbsp Cointreau

1 tbsp apricot conserve

7–8 thin slices white bread, 1–2 days old, crusts trimmed off

1 Put all the ingredients except half the orange juice and all the bread in a frying pan and simmer, stirring occasionally, until the fruits are plump and the liquid is almost gone. Be careful not to scorch it.

2 Cool the fruit mixture and remove the piece of cinnamon.

3 Continue making the Winter Pudding, as steps 3 and 4 of the Summer Pudding (opposite), using the remaining orange juice to paint over any pale bits on the pudding when it is turned out.

Per serving

Total fat (g)	1
Saturated fat (g)	neg
Unsaturated fat (g)	1
Cholesterol (mg)	0
Sodium (mg)	200
Calories	361

Makes
6 servings

FRUIT RICOTTA TIRAMISU

Full-fat Tiramisù is a wicked combination of ingredients, including mascarpone cheese, egg yolks and whipped cream. My "light" version is magnificent – you'll never miss the full-fat ingredients. Use cubes of Angel Cake (see page 143) in place of the sponge fingers to bring the fat count even lower.

INGREDIENTS

15–16 Italian sponge fingers (Savoiardi)

250g (8oz) each strawberries, blueberries, raspberries

2 ripe peaches, cubed, juices reserved

1 tsp vanilla extract

2 tbsp fresh orange juice

1 tbsp orange liqueur

550g (1lb 2oz) ricotta

400g (13oz) Quark

about 2 tbsp blueberry conserve

2 pairs Amaretti biscuits

1 Line the bottom of a 30 x 18 cm (12 x 7in) clear glass baking dish with a layer of sponge fingers.

2 Halve or quarter the strawberries and mix with all the berries in a bowl. Add the peach cubes, with their juices. Sprinkle on half the vanilla extract and the orange juice and liqueur. Toss with two spoons until thoroughly combined. Spread the fruit over the sponge fingers.

3 Put the ricotta and Quark into a food processor with the remaining vanilla extract and the blueberry conserve. Process until the mixture is smooth and fluffy.

4 Spread the cheese mixture smoothly over the fruit. Don't worry if some of the fruit shows through the cheese layer.

5 Using a kitchen mallet, crush the Amaretti biscuits and sprinkle the crumbs evenly over the cheese layer. Cover with clingfilm and chill for at least two hours before serving.

VARIATIONS

Try Cherries in Cointreau (see page 128) for the fruit layer and cherry conserve to flavour the "cream", then sprinkle sieved icing sugar and cocoa on top.

Use just the raspberries and strawberries, cover with a layer of Chocolate Cheesecake Mousse (see page 122), and top with 15g (½oz) grated plain chocolate.

Per serving

Total fat (g)	12
Saturated fat (g)	7
Unsaturated fat (g)	4
Cholesterol (mg)	47
Sodium (mg)	373
Calories	344

Makes
6 servings

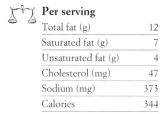

CHERRIES IN COINTREAU

I can never get enough of fresh cherries when they are – all too briefly – in season. For maximum cherriness, use a combination of all the varieties you can find.

INGREDIENTS

875g (1¾lb) cherries, halved and stoned

juice of 1½ oranges

4 tbsp lemon juice

slivered zest of ½ orange

slivered zest of ½ lemon

4 tbsp orange liqueur (e.g. Cointreau)

2 tsp vanilla extract

2–3 tbsp caster sugar

Put all the ingredients in a bowl and mix together gently with two spoons. Cover with clingfilm and leave overnight in the refrigerator.

VARIATION

Replace the cherries with blood oranges, cut into wedges, or two or three navel oranges, peeled, all pith removed and sliced into rings (not too thick).

Per serving

Total fat (g)	neg
Saturated fat (g)	neg
Unsaturated fat (g)	neg
Cholesterol (mg)	0
Sodium (mg)	6
Calories	193

Makes
4 servings

PEACH SALAD

The fragrance of vanilla with ripe peaches is magnificent. If you can't find Crème de Pêche, substitute Amaretto liqueur.

INGREDIENTS

6 large, ripe peaches

2–3 tbsp orange liqueur

1 tbsp Crème de Pêche

2 tsp vanilla extract

a few drops of lemon juice, to taste

pinch of sugar, to taste

1 Peel the peaches by putting them in a bowl of hot water for 30 seconds. Lift them out with a spoon, hold briefly under cold running water, then peel and slice.

2 Put the peaches and remaining ingredients in a bowl. Gently mix with two spoons. Omit the sugar if the peaches are very sweet.

VARIATION

Replace the peaches with ripe nectarines. Peeling is unnecessary.

Per serving

Total fat (g)	neg
Saturated fat (g)	neg
Unsaturated fat (g)	neg
Cholesterol (mg)	0
Sodium (mg)	3
Calories	112

Makes
4 servings

STRAWBERRIES IN LEMON BALSAMIC SYRUP

If you have never tried strawberries bathed in a syrup of balsamic vinegar and lemon juice, you are in for a treat. The amount of sugar depends on the quality of the vinegar, so taste as you go.

INGREDIENTS

60ml (2¼fl oz) lemon juice

1–2 tbsp sugar

1 tbsp balsamic vinegar

475g (15oz) strawberries, hulled and quartered

Put the lemon juice in a bowl. Add the sugar, stir, and leave until the sugar has dissolved. Stir in the balsamic vinegar. Toss the strawberries in the mixture until thoroughly combined. Leave, stirring occasionally, until the strawberries are bathed in a syrupy sauce.

Per serving

Total fat (g)	neg
Saturated fat (g)	neg
Unsaturated fat (g)	neg
Cholesterol (mg)	0
Sodium (mg)	8
Calories	55

Makes
4 servings

CARAMELIZED PEARS

Pears in red vermouth are heavenly. I like to serve these folded in crêpes, but they are also good as they are, topped with a ricotta or yogurt cream (see page 137), and served with an Almond Biscuit or two (see page 148).

INGREDIENTS

1 orange

1 lemon

4 firm, ripe pears

300ml (½ pint) red vermouth

1 cinnamon stick

1 vanilla pod

½–1 tbsp caster sugar

1 tbsp orange liqueur

1 Squeeze the juice of ½ lemon and ½ orange into a bowl. Peel the pears, and turn them in the citrus juices to prevent discoloration. Halve and core the pears, then dip them again. Dice the halves.

2 Put the diced pears into a heavy-based frying pan with the citrus juice from the bowl, the slivered zest of ¼ orange and ¼ lemon, the vermouth, cinnamon, vanilla pod, sugar and liqueur.

3 Bring the pears and liquid to the boil and boil, uncovered, stirring frequently, until the pears are tender. With a skimmer or slotted spoon, lift the pears out of the pan, leaving the liquid in it, and put them in a bowl.

4 Discard the cinnamon and vanilla pod. Boil down the liquid in the pan until thickened and syrupy. Pour and scrape the liquid into a small jug.

5 Return the pears to the frying pan, along with the juice of the remaining ½ lemon and ½ orange. Stir and cook quickly (but gently so that the pears do not break up) until the pears are richly glazed. Pour the red vermouth liquid into the pan and stir together.

Per serving

Total fat (g)	1
Saturated fat (g)	neg
Unsaturated fat (g)	1
Cholesterol (mg)	0
Sodium (mg)	19
Calories	256

Makes
2 servings

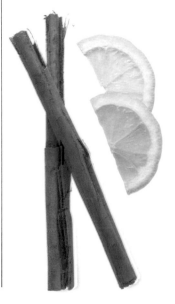

RED VERMOUTH SYRUP

A sophisticated, dark ruby, spice and vanilla-scented sauce to serve with fruit, such as pears, apricots, peaches and oranges.

INGREDIENTS

one 75cl bottle red vermouth

juice and slivered zest of 2 large oranges

juice and slivered zest of 2 large lemons

1 cinnamon stick

1 vanilla pod

250ml (8fl oz) water

4–5 tbsp sugar

1 Put all the ingredients for the syrup, except the sugar, in a heavy-based saucepan, and bring to the boil. Boil rapidly, uncovered, until the liquid has reduced by about half.

2 Take the saucepan off the heat and stir in the sugar, making sure it is completely dissolved before returning the pan to the heat. Boil the syrup for 4–5 minutes more. Remove the pan from the heat and set aside to cool completely.

3 Transfer the syrup to a bowl, cover with clingfilm and chill in the refrigerator.

4 Remove the cinnamon stick and vanilla pod from the chilled syrup. Scrape out the pulp from the vanilla pod and stir it into the syrup. (Save the scraped pod for flavouring a jar of caster sugar to make vanilla sugar.)

Per tablespoon

Total fat (g)	neg
Saturated fat (g)	neg
Unsaturated fat (g)	neg
Cholesterol (mg)	0
Sodium (mg)	3
Calories	62

Makes
About 300ml (½ pint) or 20 tablespoons

BLUEBERRY COMPOTE

Any of these compotes can be used in other desserts or served as they are with a ricotta, yogurt or fromage frais cream topping. They are also good with wedges of Angel Cake (see page 143).

INGREDIENTS

500g (1lb) blueberries

2–3 tbsp blueberry preserve or conserve

1 tbsp cornflour

juice of ½ lemon

1 tsp vanilla extract

1 Put the blueberries in a ceramic or glass baking dish. Blend all the other ingredients together smoothly, and mix with the blueberries in the baking dish.

2 Put the dish, uncovered, into a preheated oven and bake for about 15 minutes, stirring occasionally, until the mixture is thickened and bubbling.

3 Leave the compote to cool before serving.

 Per serving

Total fat (g)	neg
Saturated fat (g)	neg
Unsaturated fat (g)	neg
Cholesterol (mg)	0
Sodium (mg)	5
Calories	47

 Oven temperature
190°C/375°F/gas 5

 Makes
5 servings

PEACH COMPOTE

Another delicious compote, in which the sweetness of the fruit is countered by the addition of a little citrus juice and zest. Nectarines could replace the peaches here.

INGREDIENTS

875g (1¾lb) peaches, unpeeled

2 tbsp caster sugar

1 tbsp cornflour

2 tbsp fresh orange juice

slivered zest of ½ small lemon

slivered zest of ½ small orange

½ tsp vanilla extract

pinch salt

1 Stone and cut the peaches into chunks over a bowl so that you catch all the juices. Put the peaches and their juice with the other ingredients in a heavy-based stainless steel or ceramic saucepan.

2 Cook slowly until the liquid is thick and juicy. The fruit should be tender, but still retain its shape. Leave the compote to cool before serving.

 Per serving

Total fat (g)	neg
Saturated fat (g)	neg
Unsaturated fat (g)	neg
Cholesterol (mg)	0
Sodium (mg)	42
Calories	88

 Makes
5 servings

PLUM-PEACH COMPOTE

INGREDIENTS

625g (1¼lb) peaches, unpeeled

875g (1¾lb) plums, unpeeled

1 scant tbsp cornflour

4–5 tbsp light brown sugar

slivered zest of ½ lemon and ½ orange

1 tsp vanilla extract

3 tbsp fresh orange juice

pinch salt

1 Stone and cut the peaches and plums into chunks over a bowl to catch the juices. Put the fruits and their juices in a heavy-based stainless steel or ceramic saucepan.

2 Add the cornflour, sugar, citrus zest, vanilla, orange juice and salt. Cook slowly, stirring, until the fruit is tender, but still keeps its shape. Leave to cool.

VARIATION

For an apricot and peach compote, use 875g (1¾lb) unpeeled apricots and 300g (10oz) unpeeled peaches in place of the peaches and plums, and 1 tablespoon Amaretto di Saronno in place of the fresh orange juice.

 Per serving

Total fat (g)	neg
Saturated fat (g)	neg
Unsaturated fat (g)	neg
Cholesterol (mg)	0
Sodium (mg)	46
Calories	162

 Makes
5 servings

CLAFOUTIS

This sumptuous dessert delivers all the satisfaction of a fruit pie – with hardly any fat at all. The clafoutis, puffed up as it emerges from the oven, subsides a little as it cools. Serve it hot, warm or at room temperature.

INGREDIENTS

oil-water spray (for the flan tin)

For the batter

105g (3½oz) light plain flour

105g (3½oz) light brown sugar

3 tbsp skimmed milk powder

pinch freshly grated nutmeg

300ml (½ pint) skimmed milk

6 tbsp very low-fat natural yogurt

4 egg whites

2 tsp vanilla extract

For the fruit mixture

625g (1¼lb) peaches, stoned and cut into chunks, any juices reserved

2–3 tbsp sugar

2 tbsp orange juice

few drops lemon juice

1 tbsp apricot conserve, melted

1 For the batter, sift the flour, sugar, milk powder and nutmeg into a bowl. Whisk together the milk, yogurt, egg whites and vanilla. Pour into the flour mixture and beat or whisk until smooth. Pour the batter into the prepared tin.

2 For the fruit mixture, mix together the peaches and any juices, the sugar and the citrus juices. Scatter the mixture over the batter, leaving a 2.5cm (1in) border all round.

3 Bake in a preheated oven for 30–40 minutes until set, lightly browned and puffed. When it starts to puff and bubble, quickly and gently brush apricot conserve round the edges. Remove from the oven and set it on a wire rack.

VARIATIONS

Use nectarines instead of peaches, or a mixture of halved, stoned cherries and apricots, stoned and cut into chunks, or wedges of tart eating apples and raisins.

 Per serving

Total fat (g)	1
Saturated fat (g)	0
Unsaturated fat (g)	1
Cholesterol (mg)	2
Sodium (mg)	121
Calories	240

 Oven temperature
190°C/375°F/gas 5

 Baking time
30–40 minutes

 Baking tin
25cm (10in) non-stick flan tin, lightly oil-water sprayed

Makes
6 servings

RICE PUDDING WITH COINTREAU-SOAKED SULTANAS

This amazing rice pudding is virtually fat-free, yet it tastes so fattening! It bakes long and slow so the sugar and milk sugars caramelize – this is part of what gives the pudding its flavour and richness.

INGREDIENTS

6 tbsp sultanas (or raisins, if liked)

90ml (3fl oz) Cointreau

30g (1oz) caster sugar

1.2 litres (2 pints) skimmed milk, at room temperature

1 tsp vanilla extract

6 heaped tbsp skimmed milk powder

125g (4oz) pudding rice

1 Put the sultanas and Cointreau in a bowl and leave to soak.

2 Meanwhile, thoroughly mix together the sugar, milk, vanilla and milk powder. Stir in the rice, then add the sultanas and Cointreau.

3 Pour the mixture into a 23cm (9in) square baking dish and sit the dish in a bain marie (a roasting tin is fine). Pour boiling water into the tin so that it comes two-thirds of the way up the sides.

4 Bake in a preheated oven for about 2¼ hours, stirring after each 20–30 minutes, until the rice is tender and bathed in a thick, creamy sauce. Serve the pudding warm or cold, sprinkled with a little cinnamon or nutmeg, if liked.

 Per serving

Total fat (g)	2
Saturated fat (g)	1
Unsaturated fat (g)	1
Cholesterol (mg)	8
Sodium (mg)	264
Calories	432

 Oven temperature
150°C/300°F/gas 2

 Baking time
about 2¼ hours

Makes
4 servings

BLUEBERRY AMARETTI CRUMBLE

These elegant yet homely classics taste extremely indulgent, even though they are very low in sugar and fat. I love serving them warm, with a dollop of Cream Topping, flavoured with an appropriate fruit conserve (see page 137).

INGREDIENTS

500g (1lb) blueberries

3–4 tbsp caster sugar

1 tbsp cornflour

½ tsp vanilla extract

½ tbsp lemon juice

juice of ½ orange

pinch each cinnamon and nutmeg

6 pairs amaretti biscuits

90g (3oz) Grape Nuts cereal

1 whole egg

2 egg whites

1 Mix together in a glass bowl the blueberries, sugar, cornflour, vanilla, lemon and orange juices, cinnamon and nutmeg. Taste, and add more sugar if necessary.

2 Put the mixture into a glass or ceramic baking dish and bake, uncovered, in a preheated oven for 15 minutes, until thick, bubbly and juicy. Take the blueberries out of the oven and raise the oven temperature to the higher setting.

3 Put the amaretti biscuits and cereal into a food processor and process until they are coarse crumbs. Add the egg and whites and process until well mixed. Spread the mixture evenly over the blueberries, leaving a 1cm (½in) border all round.

4 Return the baking dish to the oven and bake for a further 7–10 minutes, until the topping is set and the juices are bubbling. Serve warm or cold.

Per serving

Total fat (g)	2
Saturated fat (g)	<1
Unsaturated fat (g)	1
Cholesterol (mg)	32
Sodium (mg)	143
Calories	177

Oven temperature
190°C/375°F/gas 5, then 200°C/400°F/gas 6

Baking time
22–25 minutes

Makes
6 servings

PEACH AMARETTI CRUMBLE

My two favourite fruits for crumbles are peach and blueberry, but apple, pear, cherry, apricot or nectarine are good too. Amaretti biscuits contain no fat or oil: the almond flavour is derived from apricot stones, not high-fat almonds. Peach Amaretti Crumble is illustrated opposite.

INGREDIENTS

juice of ½ orange

1 tbsp peach conserve

1 tbsp Crème de Pêche or Cointreau

1 tbsp Amaretto di Saronno

1 tsp vanilla extract

1 tbsp cornflour

about 5–6 peaches (750g/1½lb), peeled (see page 128) and sliced

6 pairs amaretti biscuits

90g (3oz) Grape Nuts cereal

1 whole egg

2 egg whites

1 Put the orange juice, peach conserve, liqueurs, vanilla and cornflour in a shallow baking dish, ensuring the cornflour is mixed in smoothly. Add the peach slices. Toss gently with two spoons to coat the peach slices in the mixture. Bake, uncovered, in a preheated oven for 15 minutes until bubbling.

2 Put the amaretti biscuits and cereal into a food processor and process to fine crumbs. Add the egg and the whites. Process until well mixed, then spread evenly over the peaches, leaving a 1cm (½in) border all round.

3 Raise the oven temperature to the higher setting and bake the crumble for a further 7–10 minutes, until the top is set and the juices are bubbling.

4 Serve the crumble warm. It is delicious with fruit-flavoured Cream Topping; choose an apricot or peach conserve for the flavouring (see page 137).

Per serving

Total fat (g)	2
Saturated fat (g)	<1
Unsaturated fat (g)	1
Cholesterol (mg)	32
Sodium (mg)	142
Calories	174

Oven temperature
190°C/375°F/gas 5, then 200°C/400°F/gas 6

Baking time
22–25 minutes

Makes
6 servings

RASPBERRY ALMOND CREAM TRIFLE

A trifle is such an extravagant concoction, ideal for feeding a large gathering. To make this trifle even lower in fat, replace the trifle sponges with cubes of Angel Cake (see page 143). Adding a jelly layer to a trifle is a relatively new idea; when the jelly is a fresh fruit and sherry one, I like it very much.

INGREDIENTS

For the sponge

1 x 100g (3½oz) packet trifle sponges, cubed

For the raspberry jelly

500g (1lb) frozen raspberries, thawed, and juice reserved

2 sachets (1 tbsp each) gelatine

250ml (8fl oz) orange juice

100g (3½oz) sugar

250ml (8fl oz) medium sherry

For the creamy almond layer

500ml (17fl oz) skimmed milk

45g (1½oz) skimmed milk powder

¼ tsp almond extract

1 sachet (1 tbsp) gelatine

125ml (4fl oz) hot water

pinch of salt

125g (4oz) sugar

500g (1lb) very low-fat fromage frais

For the honeyed vanilla cream topping

1 vanilla pod

500g (1lb) very low-fat fromage frais

2 tbsp runny honey

1 First make the sponge layer: arrange the sponge pieces in a single layer on the bottom of a large, clear glass bowl.

2 For the jelly, put the reserved juice from the defrosted berries into a measuring jug. If necessary, add enough water to make 350ml (12fl oz). Put the liquid in a saucepan and heat it. Sprinkle over the gelatine and leave to sponge.

3 Bring the orange juice to boiling point in a small pan and add it and the sugar to the liquid in the saucepan, stirring until the sugar has dissolved completely. Stir in the sherry. Cool slightly, then stir in the raspberries. Leave to become tepid.

4 Pour the mixture over the sponge cubes, soaking the sponge. Chill until completely set: this will take several hours.

5 For the creamy almond layer, whisk together the milk and milk powder. Rinse a heavy-based non-stick saucepan and pour out the water, but do not dry it. Put the whisked milk and almond extract in the pan and bring to just below boiling point. Meanwhile, sprinkle the gelatine over the hot water; leave to sponge.

6 When the milk is just forming bubbles on the edges, add the salt and sugar, and stir until dissolved. Whisk in the softened gelatine. Cool to tepid.

7 Whisk the fromage frais and the milk mixture together, then rub the mixture through a sieve into a bowl. Pour this mixture over the firmly set jelly. Chill for several hours until the creamy almond layer is set.

TO MAKE THE TOPPING

1 For the topping, take a small, sharp knife and split the vanilla pod lengthways. Scrape the soft pulp from each half into the fromage frais.

2 Whisk the honey into the fromage frais, and stir until the black vanilla pod seeds are evenly distributed.

3 Swirl the cream topping over the set custard. Decorate the trifle with thawed frozen raspberries and mandarin segments, if liked, before serving.

Per serving

Total fat (g)	1
Saturated fat (g)	<1
Unsaturated fat (g)	<1
Cholesterol (mg)	3
Sodium (mg)	163
Calories	353

Makes
8 servings

MERINGUE LAYER TORTE

The fillings and toppings in this meringue layer torte can be endlessly varied using other recipes in this book. For small meringues, as used in the Meringue Stack (see above and page 14), pipe 7cm (3in) circles of the mixture and bake for one hour only.

INGREDIENTS

For the meringue layers

5 egg whites, at room temperature

pinch of cream of tartar

pinch of salt

200g (7oz) caster sugar

1 tsp vanilla extract

For the fillings

1 quantity Chocolate Cheesecake Mousse, undrained (see page 122)

½ quantity cherry Cream Topping (see page 137)

125g (4oz) Cherries in Cointreau, drained (see page 128)

1 For the meringue layers, beat the egg whites with the cream of tartar and salt in a bowl until foamy. Beat in the sugar, 1–2 tablespoons at a time, until the mixture is shiny and stiff and holds firm peaks. Fold in the vanilla.

2 Line 3 baking sheets with silicone paper. Trace a 20cm (8in) circle on each. Pipe the meringue mixture to fill each circle. Bake in a preheated oven for 3 hours. Leave in the switched-off oven to cool thoroughly (at least 3 hours).

3 To assemble, spread one meringue disc with Chocolate Cheesecake Mousse. Top with a second disc and spread with cherry Cream Topping. Add the last meringue disc and spread with the mousse. Top with Cherries in Cointreau.

Per serving

Total fat (g)	14
Saturated fat (g)	9
Unsaturated fat (g)	5
Cholesterol (mg)	60
Sodium (mg)	366
Calories	508

 Oven temperature
110°C/225°F/gas ¼

 Baking time
3 hours

 Makes
6 servings

MANGO MILLEFEUILLE WITH TROPICAL FRUIT SALAD

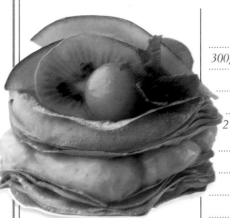

This is a very elegant dessert, with filo pastry forming the leaves of the millefeuille. Commercial oil-spray (still very low-fat) is needed here – my oil-water spray would make the pastry soggy. The mango cream filling is one of my favourites.

INGREDIENTS

For the pastry

300g (10oz) frozen filo pastry, thawed

commercial oil spray

For the mango cream

2 large mangoes (about 500g/1lb each), cubed (see below)

275g (9oz) ricotta

125g (4oz) Quark

½–1 tbsp orange marmalade

1 tsp vanilla extract

For the tropical fruit salad

2 or 3 pieces tropical fruit, such as papaya, melon and pineapple, cubed

2 blood oranges, cubed, and juices reserved

1 kiwi fruit, sliced

dash or two of vanilla extract

dash of Crème de Peche

dash of Cointreau

1 Unroll the filo pastry. Using a 7cm (3in) diameter glass as a template, cut eight circles from the stack of filo with a sharp knife. Each circular stack will consist of about eight sheets of pastry. Cover with clingfilm.

2 Oil-spray a non-stick baking tray. Take one stack of filo leaves, separate the layers and stack them, one on top of the other, on the baking sheet; spray each one lightly with oil spray as you do so. Repeat with the remaining stacks.

3 Bake in a preheated oven for 5–8 minutes until browned and a bit crisp. Flip the stacks over about half-way through the baking time. Cool on a wire rack.

4 For the mango cream, put half the mango cubes, the ricotta, Quark, orange marmalade to taste and vanilla extract in a food processor. Process until very smooth and creamy.

5 For the tropical fruit salad, mix the remaining mango with the other ingredients. Cover with clingfilm and leave to macerate for an hour or so in the refrigerator.

6 To serve, put one stack of filo circles on a plate. Cover with mango cream and top with another filo stack. Finish with tropical fruit salad and decorate with sprigs of fresh mint, if liked.

Per serving

Total fat (g)	10
Saturated fat (g)	5
Unsaturated fat (g)	5
Cholesterol (mg)	35
Sodium (mg)	244
Calories	508

Oven temperature
200°C/400°F/gas 6

Baking time
5–8 minutes

Makes
4 servings

TO PEEL & CUBE A MANGO

  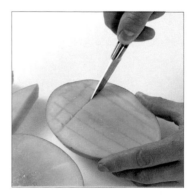 

1 Cut the mango lengthways in half, down one side of the stone. Slice down again on the other side of the stone.

2 Set aside the mango halves. Peel the skin from the flat centre section, slice the flesh off the stone and cut into cubes.

3 Score each mango half lengthways and crossways, cutting all the way to, but not through, the skin.

4 Push out the skin as if you were pushing the half-mango inside out and cut the cubes off the skins.

YOGURT CREAM TOPPING

These three toppings really rival whipped cream – they are luscious, creamy, yet low in fat. The magic ingredients are Quark, fromage frais, very low-fat yogurt (all 0% fat) and ricotta (15% fat).

INGREDIENTS

500g/1lb very low-fat yogurt

1 tbsp runny honey, to taste

2 tsp vanilla extract, or the pulp of a vanilla pod

1 Drain the yogurt overnight in a sieve lined with butter muslin. The yogurt will lose about half its volume.

2 Whisk in the honey to taste, then the vanilla extract or pulp.

Per serving

Total fat (g)	1
Saturated fat (g)	0.5
Unsaturated fat (g)	0.5
Cholesterol (mg)	3
Sodium (mg)	183
Calories	124

Makes
2 servings

YOGURT "WHIPPED CREAM"

This is my only recipe which uses uncooked egg whites and I always issue the warning: do not feed it to pregnant women, small children, the elderly or the infirm.

INGREDIENTS

250g (8oz) yogurt, drained (see Yogurt Cream Topping, above)

¼ tsp vanilla extract

2 egg whites, at room temperature

pinch of cream of tartar

2 tbsp caster sugar

1 Stir together the yogurt and vanilla extract.

2 In a spotlessly clean bowl, whisk the egg whites with the cream of tartar until they are foamy. Add the sugar, a little at a time, and continue beating until the egg whites are shiny and hold firm peaks.

3 Fold the beaten egg whites gently into the yogurt mixture, and use immediately.

Per serving

Total fat (g)	neg
Saturated fat (g)	neg
Unsaturated fat (g)	neg
Cholesterol (mg)	1
Sodium (mg)	59
Calories	49

Makes
5 servings

RICOTTA CREAM TOPPING

This lusciously creamy topping can be made with ricotta on its own, or combined with Quark or fromage frais. Use marmalade, conserve or jam instead of sugar for a wonderfully subtle flavour. Wild blueberry conserve will tint the cream a misty lilac – sheer delight.

INGREDIENTS

560g (1lb 2oz) ricotta, or half ricotta, half fromage frais or Quark

about 2 tbsp fruit preserve, marmalade, conserve or jam

1 tsp vanilla extract

Put all the ingredients in a food processor and use the pulse button to blend them together. Fruit conserves, preserves or jam give a much better flavour and texture to the topping than sugar does.

VARIATIONS

For a chocolate cream topping, replace the conserves or preserves with 1 tablespoon each sieved low fat cocoa and icing sugar.

Depending on the conserve, the topping can take on a most intriguing colour. Cherry conserve imparts a rosy blush, and blueberry an enchantingly hazy lilac colour. Orange marmalade (for an orange-flavoured topping) gives a creamy orange colour.

Per serving

Total fat (g)	7
Saturated fat (g)	4
Unsaturated fat (g)	3
Cholesterol (mg)	32
Sodium (mg)	91
Calories	144

(based on ½ ricotta, ½ Quark)

Makes
4 servings

ICE CREAMS & SORBETS

INSTANT SORBETS AND ICE CREAMS are great fun to make and wonderfully nutritious to eat. Use pieces of frozen fruits to make sorbets, add buttermilk or fromage frais to make ice creams. There is a terrific variety of sorbets here, and the chocolate sorbet is a real stunner. For the ultimate chocolate experience, however, the Deep Chocolate Ice Cream, based on a hot fudge sauce, is pure indulgence. Low-fat ice creams can also be made with different varieties of fruit or fruit combinations, and the possibilities for flavouring frozen yogurt, as a delicious alternative to ice cream, are endless.

FRUITS FOR SORBETS

Sorbets made with sweeter fruits, such as mango or papaya, only need lemon juice to sharpen the flavour, but others will need sweetening. To sweeten a sorbet, choose a conserve or marmalade that matches or complements the flavour of the fruit. Berries or cubes of fresh fruit should be frozen flat in a single layer on trays, and then stored in plastic freezer bags until needed. Drop sharply on the counter to separate the pieces.

PAPAYA   BANANA   PEACH   STRAWBERRY

RASPBERRY BLUEBERRY SORBET

Countless variations on this sorbet are possible by ringing the changes on the fruit and flavourings. For well-rounded flavour, I use honey or marmalades, conserves or jams as sweeteners – they give so much more to a sorbet than just sweetness.

INGREDIENTS

250g (8oz) frozen mixed blueberries and raspberries

2–3 tbsp orange juice

about 1 tbsp blueberry conserve

a few drops of lemon juice

1 Put the frozen blueberries and raspberries into a food processor with 1 tablespoon of the orange juice and the blueberry conserve. Process the mixture thoroughly until it is smooth and creamy. If there are any ice crystals remaining, process a little longer until they have gone.

2 Add more orange juice as needed to form a creamy consistency, along with the lemon juice and a little more conserve, if necessary. Stop processing to scrape down the sides occasionally. Serve at once.

VARIATIONS

For different yet equally delicious sorbets, replace the blueberries and raspberries with frozen sliced peaches or nectarines, pears, strawberries or bananas. To make a wonderfully smooth ice cream, use fromage frais or buttermilk instead of orange juice.

 Per serving

Total fat (g)	neg
Saturated fat (g)	0
Unsaturated fat (g)	neg
Cholesterol (mg)	0
Sodium (mg)	5
Calories	34

 Makes
2 servings

SORBETS WITH FRUIT OR CHOCOLATE *end a meal on a note of palate-tingling freshness.*

MANGO SORBET

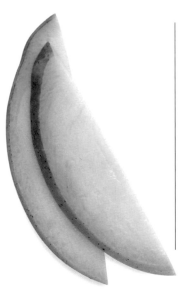

INGREDIENTS

250g (8oz) frozen mango cubes (see page 138)

a few drops of lemon juice, if necessary

1 Frozen mango whips up to a voluptuous creaminess, with virtually no added liquid. Put the frozen mango cubes in a food processor. Process until smooth and creamy, stopping to scrape down the sides when needed.

2 Taste, and if necessary add a few drops of lemon juice to sharpen the flavour. Spoon the sorbet into goblets and serve immediately.

VARIATION

Pineapple and Papaya Sorbet: replace the frozen mango cubes with 125g (4oz) frozen pineapple cubes and 125g (4oz) frozen papaya cubes.

 Per serving

Total fat (g)	neg
Saturated fat (g)	neg
Unsaturated fat (g)	neg
Cholesterol (mg)	0
Sodium (mg)	2
Calories	48

Makes
3 servings

CHOCOLATE SORBET

Serious chocolate for serious chocoholics! This sorbet uses low-fat cocoa powder, and the ice cream (below) contains high-cocoa-solid plain chocolate to ensure maximum chocolate experience, with the minimum of fat.

INGREDIENTS

250g (8oz) caster sugar

575ml (18fl oz) water

60g (2oz) low-fat cocoa powder (see page 43)

½ tsp vanilla extract

1 Gently heat the sugar and water in a heavy-based pan until the sugar has dissolved. Bring to the boil, and continue to boil for 1 minute. Remove from the heat and allow to cool slightly.

2 Put the cocoa into a bowl and stir in a little cooled syrup to make a smooth paste. Gradually stir in the remaining syrup until all the cocoa is incorporated. Stir in the vanilla and strain through a fine sieve. Set aside to cool.

3 Freeze the mixture in an ice cream maker (sorbetier), following the manufacturer's instructions, or pour into a plastic container and freeze until slushy, then process in a food processor until fluffy and store in the freezer.

 Per serving

Total fat (g)	1
Saturated fat (g)	1
Unsaturated fat (g)	neg
Cholesterol (mg)	0
Sodium (mg)	95
Calories	185

 Makes
6 servings

DEEP CHOCOLATE ICE CREAM

Chocolate lovers take note: this is a deep, meaningful, chocolate experience. To call it intensely chocolaty does not begin to describe its impact. Like the sorbet above, this ice cream is best made in an ice cream maker, though it could also be made in the freezer.

INGREDIENTS

275g (9oz) ricotta

250ml (8fl oz) skimmed milk

For the Hot Fudge Base

45g (1½oz) low-fat cocoa powder

100g (3½oz) caster sugar

8 tbsp non-fat milk powder

125ml (4fl oz) cold water

1 tsp vanilla extract

15g (½oz) plain chocolate, grated

1 For the base, sift together the cocoa, sugar and milk powder. Add the water, vanilla and chocolate, and mix to a smooth paste. Heat slowly, stirring, until bubbling gently. Leave to cool.

2 Process the ricotta and milk until smooth. Add the sauce and process again. Freeze in an ice cream maker, or freeze in a freezer, process until slushy, then refreeze (see Chocolate Sorbet, above).

 Per serving

Total fat (g)	5
Saturated fat (g)	3
Unsaturated fat (g)	2
Cholesterol (mg)	20
Sodium (mg)	187
Calories	183

 Makes
8 servings

FROZEN STRAWBERRY YOGURT

If you make the instant food processor sorbet with honeyed Yogurt Cream, the result is this splendidly fruity frozen yogurt.

INGREDIENTS

250–275g (8–9oz) frozen strawberry pieces (see page 138)

about 3 tbsp Yogurt Cream Topping (see page 137)

1 tsp vanilla extract

a few drops of lemon and orange juice

a drizzle of honey, optional

1 Put the frozen strawberry pieces into a food processor and process until slightly broken up.

2 Add 1 tablespoon of the Yogurt Cream Topping, then all the vanilla, and process until it forms a lumpy consistency.

3 With the machine still running, add another 1–2 tablespoons of Yogurt Cream Topping, and a few drops of orange and lemon juice, according to the tartness or sweetness of the strawberries. Add a drizzle of honey, if liked.

4 When the mixture forms a beautifully creamy, fluffy ice cream consistency, with no ice crystals, it is ready. Serve at once.

VARIATION

Experiment with different frozen fruits (see page 138) such as blueberry, banana, pineapple, peach or papaya.

Per serving

Total fat (g)	neg
Saturated fat (g)	neg
Unsaturated fat (g)	neg
Cholesterol (mg)	neg
Sodium (mg)	16
Calories	32

Makes
3 servings

BANANA STRAWBERRY SMOOTHIE

These amazing milk drinks are marvellously nutritious, rich and satisfying, yet they contain virtually no fat. Strictly speaking, they are not drinks because they must be eaten with a spoon. They are more of a cross between an old-fashioned soda fountain milk shake, and whipped cream, than a smoothie.

INGREDIENTS

300ml (½ pint) frozen skimmed milk

½ tsp vanilla extract

1 tbsp skimmed milk powder

1–2 tsp runny honey

frozen slices of 1 banana (see page 138)

4 large frozen strawberries, quartered

1 Partially thaw the skimmed milk (quick and easy in the microwave), until it becomes frozen slush.

2 Put the slush into a food processor (not a blender) with the milk powder and vanilla. Process until thickened and more than doubled in quantity. Drizzle in the honey.

3 Using scissors, chop the frozen banana slices in two, and dice the frozen strawberry quarters.

4 With the food processor running, add the fruit pieces, a few at a time, until well puréed.

5 Pile the creamy mixture into two tall glasses, and "drink" it with a spoon.

VARIATIONS

Mango Smoothie: substitute frozen mango cubes (see page 138) for the banana and strawberries. These drinks can also be made with other fruits, or in chocolate or mocha versions (see below).

Chocolate Smoothie: omit the fruit, and add 1–1½ tablespoons low-fat cocoa powder in Step 1. Add more honey, to taste.

Mocha Smoothie: omit the fruit. Add a sprinkling of low-fat cocoa powder, ¼–½ teaspoons instant espresso granules, and more honey to taste.

Per serving

Total fat (g)	<1
Saturated fat (g)	<1
Unsaturated fat (g)	neg
Cholesterol (mg)	4
Sodium (mg)	127
Calories	138

Makes
2 servings

BAKING

THE MOST OLD-FASHIONED AND EVOCATIVE of kitchen activities, baking fills the house with warmth, tantalizing fragrance and happiness. Baking is deeply, viscerally satisfying, and bread is a cinch to make without fat. Even splendidly rich-looking cakes can be achieved with no fat at all, not even an egg yolk.

The Angel Cake here, which is made with egg whites, is the obvious no-fat classic in this collection, but there is also a mouthwatering Carrot Cranberry Loaf to tempt the palate, as well as a rich Banana and Chocolate Loaf. Both of these loaves deliver sweet satisfaction without the fat.

CASSATA *extravagantly layers light-as-air cake, creamy filling and candied peel.*

ANGEL CAKE

Even so-called fat-less sponges are not no-fat cakes – they are made with whole eggs – but this Angel Cake is completely fat-free. It has an ethereal, delicate quality and is best served with berries and coulis or with fruit compotes. For a chocolate version, simply replace 30g (1oz) of the flour with 6 tablespoons low-fat cocoa powder.

INGREDIENTS

125g (4oz) light plain flour

275g (9oz) caster sugar

10 egg whites at room temperature

pinch of cream of tartar

1½ tsp vanilla extract

1 Sift together the flour and 105g (3½oz) of the caster sugar and set aside.

2 Beat the egg whites until foamy, add the cream of tartar and beat until they hold soft peaks. Continue beating, adding the remaining sugar 2 tablespoons at a time, until the whites are stiff and glossy. Fold in the vanilla extract.

3 Sprinkle the flour mixture over the batter a little at a time and fold in gently but thoroughly.

4 Spoon the mixture into an ungreased 25cm (10in) angel-food cake tin. Bake in a preheated oven for 30–35 minutes, or until a cake tester inserted into the centre comes out clean.

5 Invert the cake, in its tin, on an upright bottle or on an inverted funnel and cool the cake upside down for at least 1 hour.

6 Gently loosen the cake in the tin and slide it out on to a plate. Cut the cake into slices to serve, with a coulis or compote.

 Per slice

Total fat (g)	neg
Saturated fat (g)	0
Unsaturated fat (g)	neg
Cholesterol (mg)	0
Sodium (mg)	48
Calories	135

 Oven temperature
190°C/375°F/gas 5

Baking time
30–35 minutes

Makes
12 slices

CASSATA

The three layers that make up this cake are cut from a delicate Angel Cake, baked flat rather than in an angel-food cake tin. As with all the recipes in this collection, there is no compromise here – this is a fabulous cake.

INGREDIENTS

For the cake

½ quantity Angel Cake mixture (see above)

For the filling and icing

150ml (¼ pint) orange liqueur or Amaretto di Saronno

1 quantity orange Cream Topping (see page 137)

90g (3oz) candied peel, chopped

½ quantity Mocha Icing (see Dark Chocolate Icing, page 121)

1 Line a 33 x 23cm (13 x 9in) Swiss roll tin or shallow baking tin with baking parchment.

2 Make up the cake mixture as for Angel Cake, following steps 1–3 above, and spread it into the prepared tin. Bake in a preheated oven for 15–18 minutes. Let the cake cool in the tin on a wire rack.

TO ASSEMBLE THE CAKE

1 Line a 1kg (2lb) loaf tin with non-stick baking parchment, leaving an overlap at the top. Cut the cooled cake into thirds. Brush some of the liqueur over the top of each piece.

2 Put one piece of the cake, liqueur side up, in the loaf tin. Spread with half the orange Cream Topping and sprinkle over half the candied peel. Repeat with a second piece of cake and the remaining Cream Topping and candied peel.

3 Top with the last piece of cake, liqueur side down. Pull the baking parchment up over the cake and chill in the refrigerator for at least 1 hour, or overnight.

4 Unwrap the cake and ice with the Mocha Icing, reserving some for piping a decoration on top of the Cassata, if liked.

 Per slice

Total fat (g)	4
Saturated fat (g)	2
Unsaturated fat (g)	2
Cholesterol (mg)	15
Sodium (mg)	171
Calories	278

 Oven temperature
180°C/350°F/gas 4

Baking time
15–18 minutes

 Makes
10 slices

BASIC YEAST BREAD

This yeast bread is very easy to make, and the finished loaf has a delicious, crunchy bottom. It also makes an excellent pizza base (see page 145).

MUSHROOM & PESTO PIZZA

SAUSAGE & CREAMY SPINACH PIZZA

INGREDIENTS

500–625g (1–1¼lb) strong white bread flour (see method)

6g sachet easy-blend dried yeast

1½ tsp salt

about 400ml (14fl oz) warm water

skimmed milk or lightly beaten egg white, to brush the top (optional)

1 Put 500g (1lb) flour, the yeast and salt in a large bowl and mix with your fingers. Pour in the warm water, stirring continuously with a wooden spoon. When the mixture forms a cohesive mass, begin kneading in the bowl, and sprinkle the remaining flour in, a little at a time, to make a malleable dough. The amount of additional flour the dough will absorb depends on the humidity and the quality of the flour.

2 Sprinkle some flour on a work surface and turn the dough on to it. Knead rhythmically, dusting with more flour as needed, until you have a smooth, pliable, not too sticky dough. It should be elastic and extremely responsive. Press the dough with your finger – if it springs back, it is ready.

3 Form the dough into a ball and leave it to rest. Wash and dry the mixing bowl. If using an electric oven, boil a kettle of water.

4 Knead the dough briefly. Lightly flour a mixing bowl and put the dough in. Dust the top of the dough with flour and cover the bowl with clingfilm. Put the bowl into the unlit oven. If using a gas oven, the pilot light will provide a warm environment for the dough to rise, but leave the oven door slightly ajar. If using an electric oven, set a roasting tin of

boiling water on the oven floor and close the oven door. Leave for about 1 hour, until doubled in size.

5 Gently indent the dough with your finger and leave for 5–10 minutes. If the dent remains, the dough is ready for the next step.

6 Knock back the dough with your knuckles. Knead briefly and let it rest. Preheat the oven.

7 Sprinkle a non-stick baking sheet with maize meal or polenta for a crunchy bottom on the bread. Cut the dough in half, knead each piece and nudge into a bloomer shape, or roll into a flat oval then roll up into a baguette shape. Put the loaves on the baking sheet, and make three slashes across the tops with a knife. Cover with a tea towel. Leave in a warm, draught-free place for 20–30 minutes, until doubled in size.

8 Uncover the loaves. Brush with milk or egg white to glaze. Don't let egg drip on to the baking sheet. For really crusty loaves, omit the glaze, and spray the loaves with water two or three times during the first 10 minutes of baking.

9 Refill the tin on the bottom of the oven with boiling water. Bake the loaves for 40–50 minutes. When they are almost done, place them directly on the oven rack. If they appear to be browning too much on top, turn them upside down for the last few minutes. The bread is done when it is golden brown, and sounds hollow when the base is tapped. Let the bread cool on a wire rack.

Per loaf

Total fat (g)	4
Saturated fat (g)	1
Unsaturated fat (g)	3
Cholesterol (mg)	0
Sodium (mg)	981
Calories	960

Oven temperature
200°C/400°F/gas 6

Baking time
40–50 minutes

Makes
2 x 350g (12oz) loaves

TOMATO & MOZZARELLA PIZZAS

Tomato sauce and grated mozzarella cheese are classic toppings for pizza, but so is tomato sauce with no cheese, or, for that matter, cheese with no tomato sauce. Add whatever you like: strips of well-trimmed prosciutto; grilled courgettes, peppers and/or aubergine; crumbled meatballs or cooked fresh spinach; or pan braised garlic cloves – whatever takes your fancy.

TOMATO & RED
ONION PIZZA

INGREDIENTS

For the base

1 quantity Basic Yeast Bread dough (see page 144 and below)

For the topping

½ quantity Tomato Sauce (see page 66)

250g (8oz) half-fat mozzarella, grated

about 125g (4oz) pan-braised garlic cloves (see page 78)

8 vine tomatoes, sliced

handful fresh basil leaves, chopped

1 Prepare the dough up to step 7 of Basic Yeast Bread and divide into 2 or 4 compact balls. Lightly flour a work surface, then roll the dough into discs, rolling from the centre out to the edges, turning at intervals. Put the discs on lightly floured baking sheets.

2 Spread Tomato Sauce over each disc, leaving a 2.5cm (1in) border all round. Sprinkle the mozzarella, garlic cloves and tomatoes evenly over the sauce.

3 Bake in a preheated oven for 15–25 minutes, until the filling is bubbly, and the edges of the dough are puffed and golden. Garnish the pizzas with the fresh basil.

OTHER TOPPINGS

Peppers & Feta Cheese (see page 12): replace the mozzarella with crumbled half-fat Feta cheese. Top with ½ quantity Silky Stir-fried Sweet Pepper Strips (see page 71), 2 or 3 chopped black olives, and sprigs of thyme.

Sausage & Creamy Spinach (see page 12): replace the mozzarella with ricotta. Scatter over small meatballs made from ½ quantity Spicy Citrus-scented Mexican Sausages (see page 94). Top with fresh cooked spinach and grilled aubergine slices.

Tomato & Red Onion (see page 12): Tomato Sauce, ½ quantity Cherry Tomato & Red Onion Salsa (see page 61), scatter over courgette and aubergine slices, top with shavings of Parmesan.

Mushroom & Pesto (see page 12): spread over the Tomato Sauce, and top with ½ quantities of Mushrooms Made Wild (see page 74) and White Pesto (see page 63), a few strips of well-trimmed prosciutto, and 1 or 2 black olives, slivered off their stones.

VARIATIONS

Filled Pizza: divide the dough into 2 balls, then roll them into circles. Spread any pizza topping over one of the circles, lay the other one on top, and pinch the edges together to seal. Bake for 15–20 minutes.

Filled Calzone: divide the dough into 4 or 8 balls and roll out into circles. Lightly purée together 500g (1lb) each ricotta and lightly cooked spinach and spread over the circles. Add 125g (4oz) shredded half-fat mozzarella, a few slices of well-trimmed Parma ham cut into strips, and season to taste. Fold over and pinch the ends to seal. Bake for 15 minutes for small calzone, 25 minutes for larger ones.

Filled Rolls: prepare the dough as for calzone (above), then spread over the calzone filling or any pizza topping. Roll into cylinders and pinch the ends closed. Leave in a warm place to rise for 20 minutes before baking, following the timings for calzone.

Per serving

Total fat (g)	10
Saturated fat (g)	5
Unsaturated fat (g)	5
Cholesterol (mg)	19
Sodium (mg)	713
Calories	700

Oven temperature
200°C/400°F/gas 6

Baking time
15–25 minutes

Makes
4 servings, either as four 20cm (8in) pizzas, or two 30cm (12in) pizzas

PEPPERS & FETA
CHEESE PIZZA

TOMATO &
MOZZARELLA
PIZZA

WILD MUSHROOM BREAD

This loaf is best eaten a day after baking. If you do not have a food processor, the dough can easily be mixed in a large bowl. It takes a little longer to mix and knead the dough, but the result is equally successful.

INGREDIENTS

60g (2oz) dried porcini

400ml (14fl oz) very warm water

15g (½oz) fresh yeast

one 125g (4oz) sachet of instant, unseasoned potato flakes

500g (1lb) strong white flour, plus extra to dust

1 tsp sea salt

1 Soak the porcini in the water for 20–30 minutes. Drain, and reserve the soaking liquid. Rinse the porcini under cold running water and chop finely. Strain the soaking water through a coffee filter or several thicknesses of kitchen paper. Set aside the liquid and the chopped porcini.

2 Mix the yeast with 150ml (5fl oz) of the soaking liquid. Stir to dissolve the yeast.

3 Put the potato flakes, flour and salt in a food processor. Stir the remaining soaking liquid into the yeast mixture. Turn on the processor and pour the yeast mixture gradually through the feed tube. Stop occasionally to scrape the mixture from the sides of the bowl so the ingredients are well mixed. When the mixture has formed a cohesive dough, add the porcini pieces and process briefly.

4 Put the dough on a very lightly floured work surface. Knead rhythmically for 5–10 minutes, until smooth and springy. If it is sticky and difficult to handle, dust with a little flour, but bear in mind the dough should be a little sticky (too much flour will make the loaf heavy). Press the dough with your finger – if the indentation springs back, it is ready.

5 Form the dough into a smooth ball, put it in a large, lightly floured bowl, and very lightly dust the top with flour. Cover loosely with clingfilm. Place a roasting tin filled with boiling water on the oven floor. Put the bowl of dough in the oven and leave to rise for 1½ hours, until doubled in size.

6 Knock back the dough with floured knuckles and knead it very briefly. Let it rest while you lightly flour a non-stick baking sheet. Remove the tin of water from the oven; preheat the oven.

7 Form the dough into a plump, round loaf and put it on the baking sheet. Cover with clingfilm, and leave in a warm place for 30–45 minutes to double in size.

8 Fill the tin with boiling water and put it on the oven floor. Transfer the risen dough to the preheated oven. Bake for 40–55 minutes. Spray the bread with water occasionally during baking. For the last few minutes of baking, turn the loaf upside down and set it directly on the oven shelf. The bread is done when it is golden brown, and sounds hollow when the base is tapped with the knuckles. Let it cool completely (to improve its flavour).

Per recipe quantity

Total fat (g)	8
Saturated fat (g)	1
Unsaturated fat (g)	5
Cholesterol (mg)	0
Sodium (mg)	2942
Calories	2290

Oven temperature
200°C/400°F/gas 6

Baking time
40–55 minutes

Makes
one 23–25cm (9–10in) round loaf

BANANA CHOCOLATE LOAF

This cake has been very well tested, as my family and friends adore it. The only fat comes from the grated chocolate, yet the cake tastes quite rich. Serve it as it is, or spread slices with Chestnut Chocolate Cream (see page 120).

INGREDIENTS

2 very ripe bananas (they should be black!)

250ml (8fl oz) orange juice

300g (10oz) self-raising flour

1 tsp baking powder

pinch of salt

30g (1oz) plain chocolate, grated

2 egg whites

150g (5oz) soft brown sugar

1 Line a 1kg/2lb loaf tin with greaseproof paper and spray with oil-water spray.

2 Mash the bananas and orange juice together, blending well.

3 Sift together the flour, baking powder and salt. Add the chocolate and stir in the banana mixture. Whisk for 1–2 minutes.

4 Whisk the egg whites until stiff, then gradually add the sugar, whisking well after each addition. Fold the egg whites into the flour mixture until evenly blended. Spoon the mixture into the tin and smooth the top. Bake in a preheated oven for about 1 hour.

5 When the loaf has risen and is golden brown, check that it is ready by inserting a cake tester or skewer into the centre. When it comes out clean, the loaf is done.

6 Cool in the tin on a wire rack for a few minutes. Loosen the loaf carefully all around the inside of the tin, and turn out. Peel off the greaseproof paper.

7 Leave the loaf to cool then store, wrapped in foil, in an airtight container. It is best eaten on the day after it is made.

 Per slice

Total fat (g)	1
Saturated fat (g)	<1
Unsaturated fat (g)	<1
Cholesterol (mg)	neg
Sodium (mg)	165
Calories	174

 Oven temperature
160°C/325°F/gas 3

 Baking time
1 hour–1 hour 10 minutes

Makes
12 slices

CARROT CRANBERRY LOAF

My version of carrot cake is rich with fruit, but has no fat at all, not even an egg yolk. Classic carrot cake is iced with a cream cheese frosting; spread slices of this luscious loaf with one of the Ricotta Cream Toppings (see page 137) instead.

INGREDIENTS

150g (5oz) Granny Smith or other tart eating apple, peeled, cored and diced

180g (6oz) finely grated carrot

250g (8oz) sultanas or raisins soaked overnight in 250ml (8fl oz) cranberry juice

300g (10oz) self-raising flour

1 tsp baking powder

pinch of salt

1 pinch of ground cinnamon

3 tsp ground mixed spice

2 egg whites, lightly beaten

165g (5½oz) soft brown sugar

1 Line a 1kg (2 lb) non-stick loaf tin with greaseproof paper. Spray with oil-water spray. Put the apple, carrot, sultanas and juice in a saucepan. Bring to the boil and set aside to cool. In a separate bowl, sift together the flour, baking powder, salt and spices.

2 Whisk the egg whites until stiff, then gradually whisk in the sugar, making a stiff meringue.

3 Add the fruit mixture to the flour, beating well for 1–2 minutes. Fold in the meringue. Turn the mixture into the prepared tin and smooth the top. Bake in a preheated oven for 1½–1¾ hours, or until the loaf is risen and golden brown.

4 Cool the cake on a wire rack, then turn it out and remove the paper. Store wrapped in foil.

 Per slice

Total fat (g)	<1
Saturated fat (g)	neg
Unsaturated fat (g)	<1
Cholesterol (mg)	0
Sodium (mg)	154
Calories	223

 Oven temperature
160°C/325°F/gas 3

 Baking time
1½–1¾ hours

 Makes
12 slices

ANISE & FIG POLENTA CAKE

Another no-fat gem, based on a high-fat Italian classic. I love the combined flavours of anise (from fennel seeds, in this recipe) and fig in this gorgeously moist cake. Serve it in slices with Red Vermouth Syrup (see page 129).

INGREDIENTS

550ml (18fl oz) water

2 pinches of salt

1 tsp vanilla extract

180g (6oz) polenta

6 egg whites

pinch of cream of tartar

150g (5oz) caster sugar

75g (2½oz) sultanas

150g (5oz) ready-to-eat dried figs, diced

1–1½ tbsp fennel seeds

150g (5oz) self-raising flour, sifted with 1 tsp baking powder

1 Bring the water to just below the boil in a pan. Add the salt and vanilla. Pour in the polenta in an even stream, whisking well. With a wooden spoon, stir and cook until the mixture is smooth, thick and pulls away from the pan's side.

2 Whisk the egg whites and cream of tartar to soft peaks.

Whisk in the sugar, a little at a time, until the eggs are glossy and hold firm peaks.

3 Add the sultanas, figs and fennel seeds to the polenta, beating until well blended. Then add half the egg white mixture, with the flour and baking powder. Stir until well blended. Fold in the remaining egg white mixture until well incorporated.

4 Lightly oil-water spray a 20 x 5cm (8 x 2in) non-stick, loose-based cake tin and spoon the mixture into it.

5 Bake in a preheated oven for approximately 50–55 minutes, until the top is dry and slightly crackled, and a cake tester inserted into the middle comes out clean.

6 Loosen around the sides of the cake with a palette knife, and remove from the tin. Leave to cool on a wire rack.

 Per slice

Total fat (g)	1
Saturated fat (g)	neg
Unsaturated fat (g)	1
Cholesterol (mg)	0
Sodium (mg)	140
Calories	194

 Oven temperature
180°C/350°F/gas 4

 Baking time
50–55 minutes

 Makes
12 slices

ALMOND BISCUITS

These biscuits are designed to be served with sorbets, ice cream or cheesecake mousses. Best is to cut them in half, then set them into the dessert at a jaunty angle.

INGREDIENTS

75g (2½oz) amaretti biscuits

75g (2½oz) grape nuts cereal

2 egg whites

1 Put the biscuits and cereal into a blender or food processor and process to coarse crumbs.

2 Lightly beat the egg whites and mix with the dry mixture until thoroughly combined.

3 Lightly spray a non-stick baking sheet with oil-water spray. Spoon tablespoons of the crumb mixture on to the baking

sheet, leaving spaces between the heaps. Flatten gently with the back of a spoon.

4 Transfer to a preheated oven and bake for 7–10 minutes, then put the baking sheet to cool on a wire rack.

5 When the biscuits are cool, loosen all around them with a palette knife and lift them off the baking sheet. Store the biscuits in an airtight container until needed.

 Per biscuit

Total fat (g)	neg
Saturated fat (g)	0
Unsaturated fat (g)	neg
Cholesterol (mg)	0
Sodium (mg)	39
Calories	30

 Oven temperature
180°C/350°F/gas 4

 Baking time
7–10 minutes

 Makes
20 biscuits

VANILLA MERINGUE BISCUITS

Meringues make perfect, tiny, crunchy no-fat biscuits. Serve these as they are with sorbets, ice creams and mousses. Even better, serve smaller meringues sandwiched together with a rich filling. Illustrated below are heaped teaspoon-size biscuits sandwiched together with Chestnut Chocolate Cream (see page 120).

INGREDIENTS

3 egg whites at room temperature

pinch of cream of tartar

pinch of salt

150g (5oz) caster sugar

1 tsp natural vanilla extract

1 Beat the egg whites, cream of tartar and salt until foamy. Still beating briskly, add the sugar 1–2 tablespoons at a time, until shiny and stiff and the mixture holds firm peaks. Fold in the vanilla.

2 Line two baking sheets with non-stick baking parchment. Drop the mixture, in teaspoonfuls or tablespoonfuls, depending on the size you want, on the sheets, leaving 2.5cm (1in) around each one. Bake in a preheated oven for 45–60 minutes.

3 Turn the oven off. Leave the meringues in the oven for at least 3 hours, or overnight. Do not open the oven door until the time is up. Store in an airtight container until ready to serve.

 Per recipe quantity

Total fat (g)	0
Saturated fat (g)	0
Unsaturated fat (g)	0
Cholesterol (mg)	0
Sodium (mg)	365
Calories	625

 Oven temperature
110°C/225°F/gas ¼

Baking time
45–60 minutes

Makes
40 teaspoon-size biscuits (20 pairs)

BREAKFASTS

BREAKFAST IS A LOVELY MEAL: what better way to start the day than with glorious food? On busy days there may be little time for anything but a toasted quark-spread bagel, or a quick bowl of cereal and fruit, but on weekends, when breakfast often becomes brunch, it's time to pull out all the stops. It is now believed that the occasional whole egg won't hurt, but eggs are not the be-all and end-all of breakfast. Try variations of oven-baked french toast – I give two fruit-filled recipes here – satisfyingly substantial savoury clafoutis, with vegetables, or smoked haddock with crisp potatoes. What luxury!

ALMOST CLASSIC OMELETTE *cuts down on the egg yolks but does not omit them altogether.*

OMELETTE FILLINGS

An imaginative filling turns a simple omelette into a feast. The one pictured left is filled with slivers of well-trimmed prosciutto, fresh tomato and herbs. Other filling choices include many of the sauce, salsa and vegetable recipes in this book. Suggested, right, are Mushrooms Made Wild (see page 74), Glazed Fennel and Sweet & Sour Red Onions (see page 70).

MUSHROOMS MADE WILD

GLAZED FENNEL

SWEET & SOUR RED ONIONS

ALMOST CLASSIC OMELETTE

An all-egg white omelette is a daunting object. But, reduce the yolks and your omelette will be pale, but delicious.

INGREDIENTS

4 egg whites

2 whole eggs

salt and freshly ground black pepper

1–2 tsp chopped fresh herbs, optional

oil-water spray (see page 29)

about 125ml (4fl oz) filling (see Omelette Fillings, above)

1 tbsp grated Parmesan, optional

1 Put the egg whites and whole eggs into a bowl. Add a little salt (not too much, or the egg protein toughens), pepper, and the herbs, if using. Beat the eggs with a fork until well blended, about 35–40 strokes; do not overbeat or the mixture will be too thin. Lift your fork out of the mixture: when properly beaten, the egg will flow freely through the tines.

2 Spritz a non-stick omelette pan with oil-water spray, and warm it over a medium-high heat. When sizzling, with little beads of oil skittering around the pan, pour in the egg mixture.

3 Allow the eggs to set for 2–3 seconds. Then, using a wooden or nylon spatula, quickly but gently push the eggs towards the pan's centre. Work all around the perimeter of the pan, so the eggs form large, soft, moist curds.

4 Shake the pan rapidly, using sharp, definite movements, so the omelette forms an oval of fluffy, softly scrambled eggs in an envelope of coagulated egg.

5 In 10–15 seconds, when the omelette is set and cooked but still creamy and soft in the centre, and not at all browned on the bottom, spoon the chosen filling down the centre and sprinkle with grated cheese, if using.

6 Slide the omelette on to a warm plate tilted against the pan. Let the omelette fold close over the filling as it slides off the pan. The whole operation should have taken less than a minute. Serve at once.

VARIATION

Frittata: first preheat a grill. Prepare the omelette through to step 5, above. Put the frying pan under the hot grill to set the omelette top and melt the cheese, if using. Slide the frittata on to a plate, grilled side up. Cut into wedges to serve.

Per serving (no filling)

Total fat (g)	6
Saturated fat (g)	2
Unsaturated fat (g)	4
Cholesterol (mg)	193
Sodium (mg)	184
Calories	97

Makes
2 servings

MUSHROOM CLAFOUTIS

Sweet clafoutis is a French classic (see page 131). Savoury versions make festive and substantial breakfast or brunch dishes. A clafoutis puffs up dramatically, like a soufflé, and is wonderful served hot or warm.

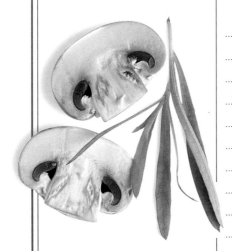

INGREDIENTS

For the filling

150g (5oz) button mushrooms, quartered

15g (½oz) dried porcini

2 sun-dried tomatoes, chopped

2 olives, slivered off their stones

300ml (½ pint) stock (see page 30)

125ml (4fl oz) dry white wine

several dashes of Teriyaki and Worcestershire sauces

For the batter

105g (3½oz) plain flour

salt and freshly ground black pepper

300ml (½ pint) skimmed milk

3 tbsp skimmed milk powder

6 tbsp very low-fat natural yogurt

1 whole egg

3 egg whites

2 tsp red pepper Dijon mustard

several dashes of Tabasco sauce

2 tbsp each chopped fresh thyme and tarragon

1 tbsp grated Gruyère

2 tbsp grated Parmesan

1 For the filling, put all the filling ingredients in a frying pan. Bring to the boil over a medium-high heat and simmer briskly until the liquid has almost evaporated.

2 For the batter, put the flour into a bowl and season. Whisk together the remaining ingredients except the cheeses. Pour into the flour and stir until just mixed with no lumps. Do not overmix.

3 Oil-water spray a 25cm (10in) non-stick flan tin. Pour in the batter. Scatter in the filling, leaving a 2.5cm (1in) border all round, and sprinkle on the cheeses. Bake in a preheated oven for 30–40 minutes until set, lightly brown and puffed. Cool on a wire rack.

 Per serving

Total fat (g)	4
Saturated fat (g)	2
Unsaturated fat (g)	2
Cholesterol (mg)	42
Sodium (mg)	304
Calories	179

 Oven temperature
190°C/375°F/gas 5

 Baking time
30–40 minutes

 Makes
6 servings

RED ONION CLAFOUTIS

Clafoutis is delicious when cooled, and this red onion version would fare particularly well at a picnic.

INGREDIENTS

For the filling

2 large red onions, halved and sliced into crescents

about 300ml (½ pint) stock (see page 30)

about 125ml (4fl oz) red wine

For the batter

300ml (½ pint) skimmed milk

3 tbsp skimmed milk powder

6 tbsp very low-fat yogurt

3 egg whites

1 whole egg

105g (3½oz) plain flour

2–3 tbsp grated Parmesan

1 Boil the onions, stock and wine in a covered non-stick pan for 3–5 minutes. Uncover, and simmer until the onions are tender. Stir in a little wine and stock to loosen any browned bits. Oil-water spray a 25cm (10in) non-stick flan tin.

2 For the batter, whisk together all the ingredients except the flour and cheese. Put the flour into a bowl, and stir in the liquid until just mixed with no lumps.

3 Pour the batter into the tin. Scatter in the filling, leaving a 2.5cm (1in) border all round, then sprinkle on the cheese. Bake in a preheated oven for 30–40 minutes until set, lightly brown and puffed.

 Per serving

Total fat (g)	3
Saturated fat (g)	2
Unsaturated fat (g)	1
Cholesterol (mg)	39
Sodium (mg)	209
Calories	167

 Oven temperature
190°C/375°F/gas 5

 Baking time
30–40 minutes

 Makes
6 servings

SMOKED HADDOCK ON A NEST OF POTATOES

I love the contrast of the smoked, flaky fish against its crisp potato bed. It would make an elegant weekend breakfast or brunch.

INGREDIENTS

250g (8oz) potatoes, scrubbed but unpeeled

2 pinches paprika

oil-water spray (see page 29)

salt and freshly ground black pepper

2 pieces of undyed smoked haddock, each about 150g (5oz), skinned and bones removed with tweezers

bunch of watercress, to garnish

1 Slice the potatoes paper-thin: using the slicer on the side of a grater is the best way of getting fine slices. Put into a colander and rinse well, then drain and dry in a tea towel. Toss the slices with a pinch of the paprika and a spritz of oil-water spray.

2 Spray a baking sheet and spread the slices out. Bake in a preheated oven for 10 minutes, then stir them, spread out again and bake for about 5 minutes more, until tender and lightly browned. They should be crisp in patches.

3 Sprinkle a pinch of paprika and a grinding of pepper over the fish. Lightly salt the potatoes and arrange in two piles on the baking sheet. Place a piece of fish over each pile of potatoes.

4 Bake for about 7 minutes, until just done. Garnish with watercress and serve with sautéed mushrooms alongside, if liked. (To sauté mushrooms, see The Morning "Fry-up", page 154.)

Per serving

Total fat (g)	2
Saturated fat (g)	neg
Unsaturated fat (g)	1
Cholesterol (mg)	54
Sodium (mg)	1149
Calories	221

Oven temperature
240°C/475°F/gas 9

Baking time
22 minutes

Makes
2 servings

THE MORNING "FRY-UP"

There is something compelling about a huge fry-up breakfast: platters of mouth-watering food, ending the long fast of the night, and stoking the mind and body for the rigours of a new day. But now it's time to indulge in the ultimate postmodern "fry"-up – all the glory with little of the fat.

INGREDIENTS

4 poached eggs

125g (4oz) button mushrooms, pan-"fried" (see method)

4 tomatoes, halved, sprayed with oil-water spray and grilled

4 toasted slices of Wild Mushroom Bread (see page 146), with fruit conserve

Spicy Borlotti Beans (see page 114)

Breakfast Sausage Patties (see method)

1 Sauté the mushrooms in 90ml (3fl oz) stock, a splash of dry sherry and a dash of Teriyaki sauce (see Techniques, page 30).

2 To make the Breakfast Sausage Patties, follow the recipe for Piquant Lemon Herb Meatballs (see page 95), but substitute half the amount of fresh sage for the mint, a whisper of nutmeg for the spices, and omit the Tabasco unless you crave fire early in the morning.

VARIATION

Postmodern Tex-Mex Breakfast: instead of toasted Wild Mushroom Bread and fruit conserve, serve a stack of warm tortillas. Serve the Spicy Borlotti Beans and leave the seasonings of the Piquant Lemon Herb Meatballs just as they are in the original recipe.

Per serving

Total fat (g)	13
Saturated fat (g)	4
Unsaturated fat (g)	8
Cholesterol (mg)	268
Sodium (mg)	1576
Calories	474

Makes
4 servings

SPOONBREAD CORN MUFFINS

These cornmeal muffins are virtually no-fat. Tender and light-as-a-feather, they rise to towering heights, and are quite wonderful for breakfast.

INGREDIENTS

165g (5½oz) cornmeal, divided in half

140g (4½oz) plain flour

½ tsp salt

½ tsp bicarbonate of soda

2 tbsp mild honey

275ml (9fl oz) very low fat buttermilk

3 egg whites, beaten until foamy

250ml (8fl oz) water

1 tsp vanilla extract

2 egg whites, beaten to stiff peaks

1 Sift half the cornmeal with the flour, salt and bicarbonate of soda. Stir the honey and buttermilk into the 3 egg whites.

2 Bring the water to the boil in a non-stick saucepan. Pour the remaining cornmeal into the water, whisking continuously. Take a wooden spoon and stir until the mixture is very smooth and pulls away from the sides of the pan (this happens very quickly). Scrape the mixture into a large bowl.

3 Stir in the egg white-buttermilk mixture and the vanilla extract. Quickly fold the sifted flour mixture into the cooked cornmeal. Whisk 2 spoonfuls of the 2 stiffly beaten egg whites in to lighten the mixture, then fold in the rest. Do not over-mix.

4 Divide the batter between 12 paper muffin cases in a non-stick muffin tin.

5 Bake in a preheated oven for 25–35 minutes, until well risen, lightly browned, and firm but springy when pressed. A cake tester inserted into the centre should come out clean.

6 Cool the muffins, still in their paper cases but out of the tin, on a wire rack.

Per muffin

Total fat (g)	<1
Saturated fat (g)	neg
Unsaturated fat (g)	<1
Cholesterol (mg)	1
Sodium (mg)	125
Calories	111

Oven temperature
190°C/375°F/gas 5

Baking time
25–35 minutes

Makes
12

CINNAMON & BLUEBERRY FRENCH TOAST

This is a good recipe for preparing the night before. Make it up to the ready-for-the-oven stage and put it in the refrigerator. Next morning, bring it back to room temperature while the oven preheats.

INGREDIENTS

180–250g (6–8oz) day-old baguette, sliced 5mm (¼in) thick

2 tbsp dried blueberries

2 tbsp raisins

2 whole eggs

2 egg whites

2 tbsp orange marmalade

500ml (16fl oz) skimmed milk

2 tbsp skimmed milk powder

½ tsp ground cinnamon

2 tbsp granulated brown sugar

1 Arrange the slices of baguette in overlapping rows to cover the bottom of a baking dish. Scatter the blueberries and raisins evenly over the bread.

2 Beat the eggs and egg whites with the marmalade. Beat together the milk and milk powder and then beat into the eggs with the cinnamon. Pour the mixture over the bread and, using a broad spatula, push the bread into the liquid.

3 Place the baking dish in a larger dish and pour boiling water in the larger dish to come half-way up the sides.

4 Bake in a preheated oven for 35–45 minutes until puffed, set and browned on top. Sprinkle over the brown sugar and serve the toast warm.

Per serving

Total fat (g)	3
Saturated fat (g)	1
Unsaturated fat (g)	2
Cholesterol (mg)	66
Sodium (mg)	315
Calories	212

Oven temperature
180°C/350°F/gas 4

Baking time
35–45 minutes

Makes
6 servings

OVEN-BAKED FRENCH TOAST WITH PEACHES

Ring the changes on this recipe with any fruit that you like. When peaches or nectarines are out of season, apples or pears work well.

INGREDIENTS

750g (1½lb) fresh peach wedges, peeled, or nectarine wedges, unpeeled

1 tbsp Cointreau

1 tsp vanilla extract

60ml (2fl oz) orange juice

180g (6oz) excellent quality day-old bread, sliced

1 whole egg

2 egg whites

2–3 tbsp peach or apricot sugar-free conserve

250ml (8fl oz) skimmed milk

2 tbsp skimmed milk powder

1 Mix the fruit with the Cointreau, vanilla and orange juice, then set aside.

2 Arrange the bread slices on the bottom of a flan dish, cutting them into halves or quarters as necessary. Pour the peaches and their juices evenly over the bread. Set aside for a few minutes to allow the juices to soak into the bread.

3 Beat the whole egg and egg whites with the conserve. Beat the milk and milk powder together and then beat into the egg mixture to make a custard. Pour it evenly over the bread and fruit, using a spatula to press the bread into the custard.

4 Put the flan dish in a larger dish, and fill the larger one with boiling water to come half-way up the sides.

5 Bake in a preheated oven for 35–45 minutes until puffed and set. Serve warm.

Per serving

Total fat (g)	2
Saturated fat (g)	neg
Unsaturated fat (g)	1
Cholesterol (mg)	33
Sodium (mg)	218
Calories	173

Oven temperature
180°C/350°F/gas 4

Baking time
35–45 minutes

Makes
6 servings

MENU IDEAS

Meticulous menu planning, using a calculator and a table of fat and calorie values, is a pleasure-deadening affair. If you practise low-fat kitchen techniques and centre your meals round plenty of vegetables and fruit, such calculations are unnecessary. Fill your meals with colour, texture and flavour, celebrate the seasons, feast days, holidays and friendship, and enjoy food for the life-giving adventure it is.

AUTUMN CELEBRATION

Smoky chicken; caramelized sweetness of roasted squash; apples and cranberries: pure autumn!

Basic Yeast Bread *page 144, with* Sweet Potato Spread *page 51 and* Butternut Squash, Ginger & Lime Puree
page 50

Smoked Rosemary Lemon Poussins
page 85

Orange-thyme Scented Wild Rice
page 115

Apple & Raisin Clafoutis
page 131

HIGH

ITALIAN VEGETARIAN FEAST

The fragrance of fennel and spices, fresh peaches and basil, wild mushrooms and balsamic: memorable.

Fragrant Vegetable Soup
page 47

Aubergine & Tomato Gratin
page 79

Tomato, Peach & Grilled Pepper Salad
page 58

Wild Mushroom Bread
page 146

Strawberries in Lemon Balsamic Syrup
page 128

Below: Fragrant Vegetable Soup

DAYS & HOLIDAYS

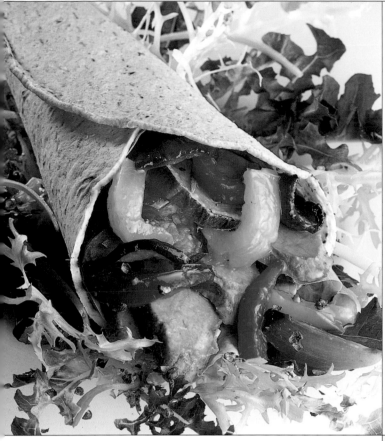

SUMMER CELEBRATION

Chilli- and lime-infused chicken with a celebration of vegetables, herbs and fruit: splendidly simple.

ROASTED VEGETABLE SALSA *page 65, with* PITTA CRISPS
page 53

....

BRAISED CHICKEN MEXICAN
page 87

COUSCOUS VEGETABLE SALAD
page 58

....

RED VERMOUTH-BATHED SUMMER PUDDING
page 126

Below: Red Vermouth-bathed Summer Pudding

MEXICAN FIESTA

New World flavours and textures: corn, chilli, roasted peppers, overflowing tortillas, dark chocolate: exhilarating.

SWEETCORN CREAM DIP *page 52 and* POTATO SKIN DIPPERS
page 53

....

SMOKED DUCK FAJITAS
page 90

....

CHOCOLATE SORBET
page 140

Above: Smoked Duck Fajitas

SPECIAL

FESTIVE SUNDAY BRUNCH

An elegant brunch begins with obligatory bagels
(no bagels, no brunch!) and combines gorgeous
textures, colours and flavours.

BAGELS *with* HERBED RAITA *page 52 and* SLICED
VINE TOMATOES

....

SMOKED HADDOCK ON A NEST OF POTATOES
WITH SAUTEED MUSHROOMS
page 153
SILKY STIR-FRIED SWEET PEPPER STRIPS
page 71

....

CARAMELIZED PEARS *page 129, with* YOGURT
"WHIPPED CREAM"
page 137

Below: Smoked Haddock on a Nest of Potatoes

VEGETARIAN BIRTHDAY BASH

Cassata makes a rich, lavish birthday cake. The
ravioli and the soup bring complexity and delicacy.

WHITE BEAN, SWEET
POTATO & FENNEL SOUP
page 49

....

GRILLED AUBERGINES & COURGETTES
page 81

OPEN RAVIOLI WITH TWO SAUCES
page 108

SALAD OF MIXED GREENS, TOMATOES
AND HERBS

....

CASSATA
page 143

Above: Open Ravioli with Two Sauces

OCCASIONS

BIRTHDAY BASH

Herby artichokes, salmon with a blazing sauce, fragrant salsa, asparagus, blueberries: sheer luxury.

STUFFED ARTICHOKE HEARTS
page 76

SALMON WITH YELLOW PEPPER &
TARRAGON SAUCE *page 104*

MANGO & FENNEL SALSA *page 61 and*
STEAMED ASPARAGUS *page 78*

SAUTE POTATOES WITH LEMON & MINT
page 73

ANGEL CAKE *page 143, with* BLUEBERRY
COMPOTE *page 130*

*Below: Salmon with Yellow Pepper
& Tarragon Sauce*

LOW-FAT CHRISTMAS DINNER

Christmas Day need not end in over consumption and exhaustion. Try an enlightened feast instead.

SPICY SWEET POTATO BISQUE *page 48*

WILD MUSHROOM PATE *page 51, with* PITTA CRISPS
page 53

DUCK BREASTS WITH CRANBERRY CHUTNEY *page 89*

SPICED GREEN BEANS WITH LIME *page 81*

GARLIC & LEMON ROASTED POTATOES *page 74*

RASPBERRY ALMOND CREAM TRIFLE *page 134*

CHOCOLATE DIPPED FRUITS *and* TRUFFLES
pages 122 and 123

Above: Chocolate Dipped Fruits and Truffles

EVERYDAY, BUT

PASTA SUPPER

Transcend spaghetti and meatballs! Family meals can shine with colour and excitement.

PENNE *with* TOMATO, GARLIC & PEPPER SAUCE
page 64

....

PIQUANT LEMON HERB MEATBALLS
page 95

ROASTED BEETROOT, ORANGE & ROCKET SALAD
page 56

....

MANGO SORBET
page 140

Below: Roasted Beetroot, Orange & Rocket Salad

ELEGANT BREAKFAST

An up-market and fanciful variation on a traditional theme: eggs, sausages, mushrooms and fruit.

ALMOST CLASSIC OMELETTE WITH VEGETABLE FILLINGS
page 151

....

BREAKFAST SAUSAGE PATTIES
page 154

MUSHROOMS MADE WILD
page 74

....

MANGO MILLEFEUILLE
page 136

Above: Almost Classic Omelette

DIFFERENT

VEGETABLE SUPPER

Rosy-tinted cauliflower, crunchy, spicy fries, carrot-
and pepper-studded beans: heavenly colour!

CANNELLINI BEAN & CHICKPEA SALAD
page 56

....

CAULIFLOWER STIR-FRIED IN RED WINE
page 69

SPICY OVEN-FRIES
page 72

GLAZED FENNEL
page 70

....

FROZEN STRAWBERRY YOGURT
page 141

Below: Cauliflower Stir-fried in Red Wine

POLENTA FEAST

Flavour-infused polenta, feisty sauce, pungent
onions, aromatic sausages: beautiful and satisfying.

GRILLED POLENTA SQUARES
page 113

ARRABIATTA SAUCE
page 66

SWEET & SOUR RED ONIONS
page 70

SPICY CITRUS-SCENTED MEXICAN SAUSAGES
page 94

....

PEACH SALAD
page 128

Above: Grilled Polenta Squares

FAT FACTS

ALL FATS, WHETHER THEY ARE highly saturated animal fats, polyunsaturated or monounsaturated oils, margarines, or the fats or oils in nuts, avocados or coconuts, provide 9 calories per gram (approximately 120 calories per tablespoon!). These are calories that are stored and metabolized into body fat in an extremely quick and efficient fashion.

So-called "low-fat spreads" may contain less fat than butter or margarine, because they have been diluted with something (water, air, or buttermilk, for example), but they still contain substantial amounts of health-threatening and calorie-dense fat. I have never understood the need for low-fat spreads. You can't really cook with them, because they are too watery. Their sole purpose seems to be to grease your bread or toast. Do you really want to add fat to your diet simply to ruin your toast and your beautiful bread?

SATURATED *VERSUS* UNSATURATED

The whole saturated-unsaturated (mono and poly) story can be incredibly confusing. To explain: it is the fatty acids in fat, defined by their chemical structures as saturated, monounsaturated or polyunsaturated, which decide a fat's type. If a fat contains a higher proportion of saturated fatty acids than of polyunsaturated, it is defined as a saturated fat – and vice versa.

Saturated fats are found mostly in animal products, and most of them are solid at room temperature. **Monounsaturated fats** are found in olive and rapeseed oils and in fat spreads made from them. **Polyunsaturated fats,** often liquid at room temperature, are found in vegetable oils, such as sunflower, safflower and soya, and in cereals, nuts and seeds.

While animals fats, including dairy fats (butter, cream, and whole milk products), lard, poultry drippings and suet, contain a high percentage of saturated fatty acids, it is interesting to note that three vegetable oils, palm oil, palm kernel oil and coconut oil, are even higher in saturates than butter.

So, if a product is labelled "made with vegetable shortening only", or "contains vegetable fat", it does not automatically follow that the product is therefore high in unsaturates. Other vegetable oils are higher in monounsaturates and polyunsaturates, although they also contain some saturates.

Since a fat with a higher proportion of unsaturation is often liquid at room temperature, some solid margarines and solid vegetable shortening are manufactured by putting highly unsaturated vegetable oil through a hydrogenation process to firm it up, so that it will be, if not hard, then "spreadable".

This hydrogenation process actually causes the oil to become saturated, in fact, saturated in a way that produces trans-fatty acids – fatty acids that are not found naturally in food, or in our bodies, and are suspected of causing even more health problems than naturally saturated fats.

In evaluating this information, just remember that all fat is equally fattening, whatever the make-up of its chemical bonds.

FATS AND HEALTHY EATING

While much solid scientific research reveals a connection between highly saturated fats and disease, especially (but not only) heart and artery disease, the unsaturated fats have also been implicated in disease, including several kinds of cancer. So, cutting back on highly saturated fats only, either for weight control or health, makes little sense. But eliminating added fats and high-fat foods makes perfect sense.

The human body needs a certain amount of dietary fat to function. But there is plenty of what you need in a bountiful diet of fish, lean meat and poultry, vegetables, fruit and grains. And the masses of these foods (plus skimmed milk powder and the oil-water spray) used in the recipes in this book will give you a full complement of fat soluble vitamins (important vitamins found in dietary fat), as well.

Epidemiological studies of the Inuit ("Eskimos") of Greenland show that fish oil seems to be heart beneficial. The incidence of heart disease among these people, who eat a diet high in fish fat, is low. Fish fat may indeed be beneficial, and fish is rich in the fat-soluble vitamins as well. It's interesting that squid and shellfish, although not particularly fatty, contain a high proportion of Omega-3 fatty acids (the components of fish fat believed to be heart-healthy). So, unless you suffer from a medical problem that precludes the ingestion of any fat, a few fatty fish meals a week are wise choices. Even the fattiest fish are relatively low in calories.

WHAT ABOUT CHOLESTEROL?

Cholesterol is a fatty substance that is manufactured in the body and is important to the body's functioning. It is the excess cholesterol levels in the blood that concern medical researchers. On the scientific level, there is much controversy. Does dietary cholesterol – that is, the cholesterol in food – affect levels of blood cholesterol? Does it contribute to heart disease? And what about "good" cholesterol and "bad" cholesterol? Does olive oil (and other highly monounsaturated oils) really raise levels of "good" cholesterol, as has been claimed?

The truth is, there are no easy answers. The whole cholesterol story, on both a medical and a scientific level, is fraught with debate and conflicting theories. On a practical level, there is no need to be too concerned. If you have cut added fats and high-fat foods from your diet, you have done much towards reducing your total blood cholesterol levels, and restoring the proper balance between so-called "good" (HDL or high-density lipoprotein) and "bad" (LDL or low-density lipoprotein) cholesterol.

It is now pretty generally believed that it is the total fat intake that may have the effect of raising blood cholesterol levels, not just frequent consumption of high-cholesterol foods. So, it seems best to ignore current media exhortations to eat lashings of olive oil or canola oil or other highly monounsaturated oils to benefit your cholesterol levels. Olive oil and the others are all pure fat. Eliminate excess fat from your life, and you will be doing the best thing possible to reduce and rebalance your blood cholesterol levels.

INDEX

ADDRESSES

Divertimenti
45–47 Wigmore Street
London W1H 9LE
tel. 0171 935 0689;
fax. 0171 224 0058
and 139–141 Fulham Road,
London SW3 6SD
tel. 0171 581 8065
Angel food cake tins and other
cookware; various flavour extracts.

Terence Fisher
Chocolate Wholesaler
Unit 23, Earl Soham Business Centre
Earl Soham Lodge, Woodbridge
Suffolk IP13 7SA
tel. 01728 685955;
fax. 01728 685956
Low-fat, unsweetened cocoa powder;
excellent quality, high-cocoa-solids
plain chocolate.

Lakeland Limited
Alexandra Buildings
Windermere
Cumbria LA23 1BQ
tel. 015394 88100;
fax. 015394 88300
Cookware, including butter muslin;
various flavour extracts, including
natural vanilla extract.

Made in America
Unit 5B, Hathaway Retail Park
Chippenham
Wiltshire SN15 1JG
tel. 01249 447558;
fax. 01249 446142
Pure natural vanilla extract.

ACKNOWLEDGMENTS

Author's Appreciation
As always, my family has provided support, love and a deep and abiding belief in my work (as I believe in theirs). Although we now live and work in separate places the bond is as strong as ever. Thank you, Steve; thank you, Shawm. A big thank you to the Fairman clan for being such good neighbours, and to my young neighbours Joe and Thomas for keeping my life lively and intellectually stimulating. How pleasant it is to become reacquainted with dinosaurs. Warm thanks to Janice Murfitt for her calm competence, to Ian O'Leary for his brilliant camera work and to Sandie Mitchel-King for her invaluable help with every facet of my work. I'm grateful to Marlena Spieler and Alan McLaughlan for their tasting input, and our far-ranging chats about food and life. I'm grateful as well to all my Roman Road chums. I wouldn't trade life on the Roman for any other place on earth! Hugs and kisses to Katie Ashley, my best Roman Road friend of all, who is always there for me, and to Janet Tod whose work on canvas embodies all that I feel about food, pattern and colour. What a privilege it is to have such friends! And, finally, heartfelt and grateful thanks to

Jeanette Hoare, Tonianne Kempson and Brenda Huebler who all, in their own way, help to keep chaos at bay. And Jeanette: you are such a pleasure to feed. May your enthusiasm never dim. The oven-baked Blueberry French Toast is especially dedicated to you.

Dorling Kindersley would like to thank Hannah Attwell for design assistance, Tracey Clarke for initial design work, Lorna Damms and Julia Pemberton Hellums for editorial assistance, Jasmine Challis for the nutritional analyses, Hilary Bird for the index, Oona van den Berg for home economy, Emma Brogli for photographic assistance and Emma Murfitt for hand modelling.

Picture Credits:
Photography by Ian O'Leary, except: Dave King 30 top; Patrick McLeavy 26–27, 28, 29, 30 bottom, 31 (except top), 32, 33, 34 (except top), 35 (except middle row, first two pictures), 36 (except top), 37, 126 top; David Murray 136 bottom; Clive Streeter 7, 9, 10–11, 14, 15, 21, 60, 82–3, 121, 135, 136 top.